house rabbit primer

understanding and caring for your companion rabbit

lucile c. moore

SANTA
MONICA
PRESS

Published by:
Santa Monica Press LLC
P.O. Box 1076
Santa Monica, CA 90406-1076
1-800-784-9553
www.santamonicapress.com
books@santamonicapress.com

Printed in the United States

Santa Monica Press books are available at special quantity discounts when purchased in bulk by corporations, organizations, or groups. Please call our Special Sales department at 1-800-784-9553.

ISBN 1-891661-50-7

Library of Congress Cataloging-in-Publication Data

Moore, Lucile C., 1952-
  A house rabbit primer : understanding and caring for your companion rabbit / Lucile C. Moore.
    p. cm.
  Includes bibliographical references and index.
  1. Rabbits. I. Title.

SF453.M625 2005
636.932'2--dc22

2004029784

Design and production by Future Studio Los Angeles

table of contents

part i. house rabbit care and behavior

chapter 1

chapter 2

chapter 3

chapter 4

chapter 5

part ii. rabbit health and medicine

To my mother, who loves rabbits;
my father, who loves writing;
and in memory of
Bunnyman, Mr. Tim, and Sweetie Pie,
for the joy they brought to my life.

house rabbits. although greatly increasing in popularity, are still unusual pets. New human companions of these delightful animals often find themselves at a loss when attempting to interpret their rabbits' behavior. While there are some books available on rabbit care, few are specific to *house* rabbit care. The Internet abounds with rabbit Web sites, some of which have good information on house rabbits, while others provide erroneous and misleading information. The search for knowledge can become frustrating.

I know, because I went through it myself when I began having companion rabbits in my home. My frustrating search, shared by almost every other house rabbit owner I met, led me to write this guide for understanding and caring for rabbits in the home. I hope it may save new bunny parents from making some of the errors I made, and provide a useful reference volume for the more experienced rabbit owner.

House rabbits are sometimes referred to as "pets" and their caretakers as "owners" in this book because that is still the prevalent usage. But as every person who shares their home with one of these marvelous animals knows, house rabbits are companions in the truest sense of the word.

I owe many people debts of gratitude for their assistance in putting this book together. I have found that rabbit people tend to be most generous with their advice and time. But I am particularly grateful to the following people:

William E. Kurmes, DVM, for reviewing the information in the medical section. Any errors are entirely my own.

Dave Stewart, for bringing Bunnyman into my life

and thereby starting me on my rabbit journey.

Everett and Melissa White for their technical assistance and for trying an early draft of the book out on their two house bunnies, Peanutbutter and Flower.

John and Marie for their generosity in giving their time and sharing their experiences.

Kim Dezelon, Stephen Guida, Velly Oliver, and the other dedicated volunteers with Brambley Hedge Rabbit Rescue for their time and photo contributions.

Valerie Fox for sharing her pictures of Bailey.

Timiae Harper, Janelle Newby, and Sunny Oaks Flemish Giants for generously contributing breed photos.

LUCILE C. MOORE, PH.D.
March 2004

part one

house rabbit care
and behavior

why a pet rabbit?

without question. house rabbit owners are members of a pet elite. They have the unusual ability to find companionship, amusement, and boundless joy in sharing their lives with an animal many others see as boring, timid, stupid, or unresponsive. They are self-confident enough to remain unfazed when discovered crawling on the floor, rubbing noses with their pets, jumping up and down, or even running in circles and shaking their heads in imitation of a rabbit gone "binky." Friends and relatives shake their heads in disbelief, raise their eyebrows and wonder—silently or aloud—why anyone would want a pet *rabbit* when they could have a nice affectionate dog or warm lap cat.

Who could resist sharing their life with such an appealing companion?

Yet pet rabbit owners remain stubbornly loyal and are slowly but consistently winning others over to their passion. Although U.S. households with pet rabbits number considerably fewer than those with cats and dogs, their ranks are steadily increasing. According to the American Pet Products Manufacturers Association, rabbits overtook hamsters as the most popular small companion animals in the U.S. in 1996–1997, and have since continued to widen their lead.

What is it about these apparently timid and quiet animals that gained the affection, loyalty, and admiration of people as different as writer and naturalist Beatrix Potter and actor Steve McQueen? What they had discovered, and what many people today are discovering, is that behind the deceptively soft and timid appearance of the rabbit is an animal that is wonderfully affectionate, impeccably clean, entertainingly playful, and always beguiling. Still, it must be said that rabbits are not for everyone. In addition to the aforementioned qualities, they can also be extremely stubborn, destructive, demanding, and temperamental.

The failure to understand the less appealing aspects of rabbits' personalities beforehand is leading to an increase of unwanted and abandoned rabbits even as others discover the joys of rabbit ownership. Rabbits *look* so cuddly and sweet one naturally expects them to act that way. When new owners find to their surprise that their rabbit doesn't always want to sit in laps and cuddle, chews holes in expensive clothes, doesn't get along with very young children, rips wallpaper off the wall, and bites when ignored, they are taken aback. Faced with this unexpected behavior, the new rabbit owners may feel aggrieved and disappointed and no longer want their pets. Some of these misunderstood rabbits end up alone and unhappy in backyard hutches, others are taken to shelters, and, tragically, some are turned loose to fend for themselves. These last have almost no chance to survive—when they freeze at the sight of danger their unnatural colors make them stand out, an easy target for predators, and they are without the social support of other wild rabbits and the protection of their warren.

But for the person willing, ready, and able to accept rabbits for what they are, they make wonderful pets. Rabbits can be ideal for apartment dwellers, as they are clean, quiet, and don't need tons of space. They are also good pets for people who have to work every day, because they readily adapt to being in a cage during daytime work hours as long as they are let out to play mornings or evenings. Are you tempted? Following is a list of frequently asked questions for people who have never had a pet house rabbit but would like to know more.

ten frequently asked questions ●

1● Is a rabbit more like a cat or a dog?
Some rabbit owners become annoyed when asked this question, but I find it natural that a prospective owner would want to understand the rabbit in the context of the two most popular pets. The answer is, like both and like neither. Like cats, rabbits are insatiably curious and impeccably clean. Like dogs, rabbits are often (not always) demonstrably affectionate and endearingly clumsy. A major difference from both, however, is that while cats and dogs are both predators, rabbits are everyone's favorite lunch. This basic difference in their position in the scheme of things in the wild affects their

behavior in one's home. Rabbits *cannot* be disciplined or otherwise treated the same way as cats or dogs.

2. Aren't rabbits some kind of rodent?

No. Although once included in the mammalian order Rodentia, rabbits were reclassified in the mid 1900's and put into the order Lagomorpha, which includes rabbits, hares, and pikas (a small rabbit-like mammal of the Americas). Some researchers, using sophisticated protein sequence analyses, have even suggested that rabbits are actually much more closely related to primates than to rodents! (Although other researchers disagree.)

3. Are rabbits easy to take care of?

Another yes and no answer. Rabbits are usually most active during the morning and evening, so they do adapt to being kept in a cage during the day. However, rabbits are social animals, and must be given a great deal of attention to thrive. They need to be groomed occasionally, and care must be taken in feeding them, as they have easily upset digestive systems. And while they are naturally clean animals, in one's home they depend upon the owner to remove soiled litter and keep their food and water fresh. Rabbits also have fragile skeletons, and require careful handling to avoid broken backs and other injuries.

4. Can you litter-train a rabbit?

Again, yes and no. Rabbits, particularly older ones, can be trained to urinate in a litter box and to leave most of their droppings in a litter box. However, rabbits will probably always leave a few territorial droppings here and there, and they tend to lose a few when they are very excited. These droppings are dry and odorless, and easily cleaned up with a hand-held vacuum.

5. I've heard rabbits chew on everything — is this true?

An emphatic yes! Rabbits' teeth grow continuously all their lives and they have to chew things to keep their teeth worn down. Providing toys and chew sticks can help to reduce destructive chewing on books, furniture and other items (see Chapter 3), but rabbit owners should resign themselves to a certain amount of destruction of property. To those who are captivated by rabbits' enchanting personalities the loss of a few pairs of shoes and maybe a couple of choice antiques seems a small price to pay for the pleasure of their company.

6. Can rabbits get along with cats and dogs?

Most rabbits can learn to get along with other family pets, although some rabbits are uneasy around ferrets. Cats in particular may form strong bonds with rabbits. However, a rabbit should *never* be left unsupervised with any cat, dog, or other predatory pet, no matter how long and how well they have gotten along with the rabbit. Too many rabbits end up seriously injured or dead when left unsupervised for even a short while with the family cat or dog. Cats and dogs also carry certain organisms which can be dangerous to rabbits, and some precautions must be taken with sanitation.

7. Are rabbits good pets for children?

For very young children, no. Rabbits are often frightened by the excited shouting and sudden movements of young children. Rabbits may suffer broken backs if held and handled by a child too young to understand how to do so properly. Rabbits can, however, make excellent pets for children 8 years of age and older.

8. Do rabbits bite?

Yes. Even good-natured rabbits sometimes communicate with small nips. Rabbits will also scratch and bite if they are held against their will, or frightened. A few rabbits (usually as a result of the owners trying to discipline the rabbit like they would a cat or dog) become aggressive and attack viciously.

9. How long do rabbits live?

It depends on the size of the rabbit. Very small rabbits tend to have shorter lives of 5 to 6 years. Average-sized rabbits (about 6–12 pounds) may live 8 to 12 years or more. Very large rabbits (over 14 pounds) may have shorter lives, about 6 to 10 years. These life spans presuppose good health and proper care of the rabbit, of course.

10. What is the difference between hares and rabbits?

Rabbits and hares are in the same mammalian family, but different genera, and do not interbreed. Hares differ from rabbits in that they have larger heads, a larger volume of blood,

A rabbit's split lip is one of their most noticeable facial features.

longer ears and legs. They both have split lips, but the rabbit has a membrane near the top of the split that covers the gums. Rabbit young are born naked with eyes closed; hare young furred with eyes open. In general, hares are more adaptable and live on top of the ground; many rabbits burrow and have more restricted ranges. You can't always tell which is which by common names—jackrabbits and snowshoe rabbits are in fact hares, and Belgian Hares are rabbits.

a brief history of rabbits

The ancestors of rabbits originated in the Western Hemisphere and from there migrated to Asia and then Europe. Lagomorph fossils have been found in late Eocene and early Oligocene deposits in North America, Europe, and Asia. The earliest rabbits of the genus *Oryctolagus*, from which modern domestic rabbits are descended, probably originated in Iberia before the Pleistocene and moved northward into Europe. Hares and rabbits were both widespread in Europe by the mid-Pleistocene, but after the Pleistocene glaciation rabbits were pushed southward back to the Iberian Peninsula. The Phoenicians discovered them there about 1000 BCE and took some back to their country. From there rabbits began to spread around the Mediterranean.

Hares were a staple food of the Roman armies. The Romans kept hares in large walled enclosures called *leporaria*, which were sometimes even roofed to keep predators away. About 100 BCE, Varro, a well-educated Roman interested in agriculture, suggested that the similar rabbits introduced by the Phoenicians be kept in the same manner. This idea was adopted, although the walls of the *leporaria* had to be extended further underground to contain the burrowing rabbits. Rabbits were in Italy by 230 CE, and the Romans introduced them to other countries around the Mediterranean and to Normandy. It has been supposed that some of the burrowing rabbits escaped from the walled *leporaria*, and that it was through this means that wild colonies around the Mediterranean became established.

It was to the medieval monks of France, however, that we owe today's domestic rabbit. The flesh of certain rabbits was not considered meat, and monks were allowed to eat it even during Lent. In order to have this form of sustenance handy the monks kept rabbits in hutches and at some time between 500 and 1000 CE began selectively breeding them. Rabbits were prized for their fur as well as their meat, and by the 1500s were being bred for colors. A painting by Titian from 1530 (Madonna with the Rabbit) depicts an all-white rabbit. Black, spotted, yellow, and gray rabbits were developed by the end of the 1500s.

The captive, selectively bred rabbits of the monks were slowly introduced to the rest of Europe. Some of these domestic rabbits escaped, managed to survive, and began to slowly colonize the countryside. Although they belong to the same genus and species (*Oryctolagus cuniculus*), modern wild rabbits of England and northern Europe are actually more closely related to domestic rabbits than to the true wild rabbits of Spain and Portugal. The cottontail rabbits of North America belong to a different genus (*Sylvilagus*) and are true wild rabbits.

Rabbits perhaps first enjoyed popularity as house pets in Italy during the Renaissance. Pet rabbits belonging to members of the upper classes, especially women, were much pampered and loved pets. Cherished rabbits were buried in tombs and their disconsolate owners commissioned funeral odes to be composed upon their death.

Keeping rabbits as pets was not restricted to Europe. A Sioux tale tells of a young girl who had a rabbit she loved so much that she made moccasins for it and slept with it in her blanket at night. The mother of the little girl was also fond of the rabbit—so much so that she called it her grandchild. When the rabbit was killed by a young boy who hit it in the head with a stick, the girl cut her hair in mourning. The "grandmother" helped her daughter hold a mourning feast at which blankets, knives, and other valuables were given away in honor of the rabbit. Finally, he was wrapped in a robe and left on a high scaffold.

Hares as well as rabbits have been kept as house pets. The 18th century poet William Cowper kept three leverets (young hares) as pets. He made house cages for them and let them out to run loose in his parlor each evening. One evening Cowper made an important official come up the back stairs rather than allow him to disturb the hares. Cowper's favorite hare would sit in his lap, lick his hand, and stand up to chew on his hair. The hares became Cowper's most beloved pets, and although one died young, the other two lived 8 and 11 years.

Still, those who kept rabbits or hares as pets were a small minority. Rabbits continued to be raised primarily for food and fur until about the mid 1800s. At this time rabbits began to be bred for fancy (show) purposes. One rabbit in particular, the Belgian Hare, was responsible for a surge in the popularity of breeding rabbits for their appearance, as was the bicolored Dutch. The appealing appearance of these rabbits led some people to keep them as pets as well as for show. Author and naturalist Beatrix Potter owned several rabbits over her lifetime, including a wild rabbit, a Belgian Hare, a silver-gray, and a chocolate-colored rabbit. One she trained to a leash and carried with her in a wicker basket when she traveled.

As the 20th century progressed, more and more breeds of rabbits were developed, and greater numbers were being kept as pets. A painting by Scottish artist David Fulton (1848–1930) depicts a young girl lying on the grass with three Dutch rabbits nearby. A 1950's novel by the Japanese writer Junichiro Tanizaki mentions rabbits kept as pets in the entry hall of a house. However, most rabbits that were kept as pets were kept outdoors in hutches and rarely, if ever, let into the house. Then in the 1970s three lop breeds were introduced to the United States: the French Lop, Mini Lop, and Holland Lop. These breeds became extremely popular, and their appealing, puppy-like appearance tempted more owners to keep them indoors as part of the family.

With the increase of their popularity as house pets, more information became available on the personality and needs of domestic rabbits. In the 1980s and 1990s, several groups were founded with the purpose of promoting the welfare of domestic rabbits. Other groups rescue rabbits from shelters and attempt to find them homes with people who understand and appreciate this unusual pet. As more and more people discover the unique animal called the domestic rabbit, the 21st century promises to be the best one yet for this most delightful of house pets.

choosing a rabbit

so you have decided to risk having your antiques destroyed and your remote control demolished and intend to join the elite community of house rabbit owners. But you're not sure what kind of rabbit you want, or what sex, or how old, or even how many you want. And where would be the best place to find one?

what breed is best?

At the time of this writing, there are 45 rabbit breeds officially recognized by the ARBA, or American Rabbit Breeders Association. (Countries other than the U.S. will have their own recognized breeds, which may not be the same.) Wherever you end up finding your rabbit —and I personally would hope you might give a shelter rabbit a second chance at life—chances are it will be one of these breeds. There are a few mixed-breed rabbits available, but even these rabbits will probably have fairly recognizable ancestry. Most of the breeds were originally developed for one of four purposes—meat, pelt, wool, or fancy (show), but any of them can make a good pet. I don't think there is a single breed of rabbit about which someone has not claimed it makes the absolute best pet for one reason or another!

Given that any breed of rabbit can make a good pet, two factors to take into consideration are the size of the rabbit and the amount of care it requires. While larger rabbits may make affectionate, laid-back pets, they do require larger cages, more room to exercise, and more feed. Very large breeds can be more difficult to handle and may be prone to certain problems, such as sore feet (often referred to as "sore hocks"). Wool breeds such as the Angoras and Jersey Wooly require considerable daily grooming. The smallest breeds can be rather high strung and don't do as well with younger children as do some of the slightly larger and hardier breeds like Dutch and Mini Lops.

I have divided the following list of breeds into five size categories. The weight range given is not the show weight requirement but a range into which an adult of that breed would be likely to fall (it is not absolute—any individual could fall above or below the range). Female rabbits (does) are often somewhat larger than the males (bucks), so use the top end of the weight range for females and the bottom end for males. If there are any special care requirements for the breed I have listed them following the description. Breeds marked with an asterisk are not yet fully recognized by the ARBA. Those who show rabbits use the term "variety' to denote the different fur colors; I have tried to avoid this word as well as other technical terminology used by professional rabbit breeders.

Smallest Rabbit Breeds
(mature weight usually less than four pounds).

American Fuzzy Lop: three to four pounds. These small rabbits have a large, flattened "bulldog" face and lopped ears, and look somewhat like a Holland Lop with long fur. They have been bred in many different colors. This is a wool breed, and will require extensive daily grooming and a special diet.

Britannia Petite: two to 2½ pounds. These tiny, compact rabbits have relatively narrow heads and a trim, arched body line. Ears are medium long and erect. Colors include white, black, otter, chestnut, agouti (like a wild rabbit), and sable marten. Experienced rabbit breeders have claimed these rabbits have a tendency to be more hyper and nip more often than other breeds, and that they require especially careful handling because of the delicate arched body type.

Dwarf Hotot: two to three pounds. These little rabbits have a very striking appearance—they are all white except for a ring of black around the eyes, which makes them look like white rabbits with black eyeliner. They have compact, rounded bodies and short, upright ears.

Himalayan: 2½ to 4½ pounds. White rabbits with ears, nose, feet, and tail colored black, blue, lilac, or chocolate. Body is long and narrow with a narrow head and rather short erect ears.

Holland Lop: 2¾ to four pounds. Head is slightly flattened, body is short and looks massive.

They have lopped ears and a prominent "crowns" (the ridge of cartilage between the ears). These popular rabbits come in many colors and have soft, fine fur.

Female Holland Lop.

Jersey Wooly: 2¾ to 3½ pounds. Body is rounded and compact. The fur on the face and upright ears is short; the rest of the body has long, dense fur. They have been bred in many colors. These rabbits require extra time for grooming and special diets.

The Jersey Wooly.

Lionhead*: three to 3¾ pounds. This breed originated in Belgium but has been developed in England. Body is well-rounded. Fur on body is dense and of medium length; fur two to three inches long forms a mane around the head. Lionhead rabbits with both lopped and upright ears

Lionheads.

are being developed at the time of this writing, but only one or the other is likely to be accepted by professional breeder associations.

Mini Plush Lop*: 2½ to 3½ pounds. This breed was created in the late 1990s by Devie D'Anniballe by mixing the Mini Rex, Mini Lop, and Holland Lop. It is not recognized by ARBA at the time of this writing. The fur is like that of a rex, the appearance between that of a small Mini Lop and Holland Lop. Personality usually affectionate.

Mini Rex: 2¾ to 4½ pounds. The Mini Rex rabbit has a compact body with narrow shoulders; short, thick, upright ears, and a rex coat. Rex coats have guard hairs which are fine, straight, and no longer than the under-

Mini Rex doe. B&B's Lay.

hairs, resulting in a plush coat that looks and feels somewhat like velvet. They have been bred in many colors.

Mini Satin*: three to 4½ pounds. Several people in the United States are working to develop a small rabbit with the fur and body type of the eight to 10½ pound standard Satin.

Netherland Dwarf: 1¾ to 2½ pounds. These rabbits have compact, rounded bodies, large heads, short necks, and short, erect ears. Fur is glossy and dense and comes in many colors. Like the Britannia Petite, some rabbit owners claim these are more prone to nip than other rabbits and might be less suitable for children.

Polish: two to 3½ pounds. Compact body; short, thick, upright ears. Fur is short and dense and is black, blue, chocolate, white, or broken (color is in splotches on white background).

Small Rabbit Breeds
(mature weight of bucks and does usually between four and seven pounds).

Dutch: 3½ to 5½ pounds. Compactly built rabbits with well-rounded hindquarters. There is a blaze of white on the face, and the front feet, upper torso, and toes to mid-foot of the hind feet are also white. The rest of the body is black, blue, chocolate, tortoise, steel, or gray. Ears are generally large and upright. This breed usually does well with children.

Black Dutch.

English Angora: five to seven pounds. Thick wool covers the entire rabbit, including the face and the stand-up ears, giving it the appearance of a large fuzz-ball. They have been bred in many colors. These rabbits require special diets and extensive daily grooming.

Florida White: four to six pounds. Short rounded body, rounded head and short erect ears. They are white with ruby (pink) eyes.

Havana: 4½ to 6½ pounds. Black, blue, or chocolate colored. Body is short with wide shoulders and hind-quarters. Head is narrow, ears medium-long and upright.

Mini Lop: 4½ to 6½ pounds. Body is massive, thick-set, with short neck. Ears are lopped, and the ears and crown form a horseshoe shape on the top of the head. Fur is thick and dense. Many different colors have been bred. A sturdy breed excellent for children.

Male Mini Lop.

Silver: four to seven pounds. Black, brown, or fawn rabbits with white ticking (silvering). Body relatively long, head narrow, ears long and erect.

Standard Chinchilla: five to seven pounds. Compact, chubby-looking body of medium length. Ears long and upright. Each hair of fur has three bands of different colors: blue at the base, pearl in the middle, and black at the top.

Tan: four to six pounds. Belly, chest, flanks, inner part of front and hind legs, triangle at nape of neck and underside of tail are tan. The rest of the fur is solid black, blue, chocolate, or lilac-colored. Body is narrow and thin, medium-long and racy looking. Ears are large and upright.

Velveteen Lop*: five to 6½ pounds. Body is mandolin-shaped, chest is full and rounded. The ears are lopped and measure from 14 inches tip to tip. Fur is like that of rex rabbits. (This breed has been described as a miniature English Lop with rex fur.) It is being bred in several colors. At the time of this writing the breed has been presented at the ARBA but has not yet completed the recognition process.

Medium Rabbit Breeds
(mature weight usually between six and 10½ pounds).

American Sable: seven to 10 pounds. Nose, ears, feet, and tail very dark brown, body a sepia color. Body is medium long and full, head narrow, and ears long and erect.

Belgian Hare: six to 9½ pounds. This rabbit has a lean racy body that looks more like a hare's than a rabbit's. Large upright ears. Some rabbit owners claim it is more prone to bone fractures if mishandled, due to the body type.

Californian: eight to 10½ pounds. White with black ears, nose, feet, and tail. Full-bodied with medium-length, upright ears.

English Spot.

English Spot: six to eight pounds. Racy body, long erect ears. Butterfly mark on nose, cheek spots, line down the back, and side spots are colored, body is white. Some people claim it has a rather nervous temperament.

French Angora: 7½ to 10½ pounds. Medium-long rounded body, ears long and erect. Face, ears, and front feet have short fur; rest of body has very long wool. Many different colors have been bred. This rabbit must be fed a special diet and carefully groomed every day.

French Angora. AA's Bigote.

Giant Angora: 8½ to 9½ pounds. These rabbits are white with ruby eyes. Compact and rounded with long wool on entire body, including tail, feet, and upright ears. This rabbit has the most wool of any, because of a dense undercoat. It requires extensive daily grooming and a special high-protein diet.

Harlequin: seven to 9½ pounds. This striking rabbit originated in France. The body is banded with two colors, and the head is also two colors. It has a medium-length

31

body with rounded hindquarters, a rounded head, and long, upright ears.

Hotot: eight to 11 pounds. Like the Dwarf Hotot, this rabbit is white with black ringing the eye. Body is rounded and thick, head is narrow, ears are medium-long and upright.

Lilac: $5\frac{3}{4}$ to eight pounds. This rabbit is dove-gray with a pinkish tint. It has a medium-sized body with a somewhat narrow head and medium-long erect ears.

Lilac. Wooley Booger's Lista.

Palomino: eight to 10 pounds. This rabbit has beautiful fur of a golden or lynx color. Body medium-length, ears medium-long and upright.

Rex: $7\frac{1}{2}$ to $10\frac{1}{2}$ pounds. Medium-sized, well-rounded body with large erect ears. Coat is as with Mini Rex, looking and feeling like plush velvet.

Rhinelander: $6\frac{3}{4}$ to 10 pounds. This is a tricolored rabbit, white with spots of black and orange. It has a rather racy body with a narrow head and long upright ears.

Satin: eight to $10\frac{1}{2}$ pounds. The coat of this rabbit is dense, soft, and has a sheen to it. It has been bred in many colors. The body is medium, slightly narrower in shoulders and head, ears medium-long and erect.

Satin Angora: 6½ to nine pounds. This rabbit has long, fine, glossy-appearing wool covering all its body but the head and the upright ears. It requires extra grooming and a special diet.

Male Satin.

Silver Marten: 6½ to 9½ pounds. Black, blue, chocolate, or sable fur with chest, shoulders, flanks, hindquarters and limbs dotted with long white-tipped guard hairs. Body is medium-sized and well-rounded, ears long and erect.

Large Rabbit Breeds
(mature weight usually nine to 12 pounds).

American: nine to 12 pounds. Slate blue or white. This rabbit has well-rounded hindquarters, narrow shoulders, and long erect ears.

American Chinchilla: nine to 12 pounds. Medium-length body with well-rounded hindquarters. Base of each hair is slate blue, intermediate band is pearl, top band is black. Ears are long and upright.

Beveren: eight to 12 pounds. Pear-shaped body, long erect ears, dense coat of black, blue, or white.

Champagne D'Argent: nine to 12 pounds. This unusual rabbit has a coat that changes gradually from black when very young to silver as an adult. Body is medium-length, full and round; ears are long and erect.

Cinnamon: 8½ to 11 pounds. Cinnamon-colored rabbit with gray ticking across the back. Body is medium length, well rounded; ears are large and erect.

Creme D'Argent: eight to 11 pounds. Orange-silver-colored rabbit. Medium-length rounded body, ears medium-long and upright.

English Lop: nine to 12 pounds. Hindquarters are rounded, shoulders and head narrow. The ears are lopped and extremely large, often measuring 24 inches from tip to tip. This rabbit requires extra care because of the ears, which are susceptible to disease and injury. It is not recommended for a first-time rabbit owner.

French Lop: 10 to 14 pounds. The largest of the lop breeds. This rabbit has a massive, well-muscled body with a wide head and thick, wide, lopped ears. The French Lop has been bred in many different colors and is a favorite companion rabbit of

French Lop.

many because of its laid-back and affectionate personality.

New Zealand: nine to 12 pounds. Fur black, red, or white. Body is medium-sized and well-rounded. Ears are medium-long and upright. One of the rabbit breeds often used in laboratories, it makes an excellent pet.

Silver Fox: nine to 12 pounds. Fur is black with silver-white hairs throughout coat. Body is of medium length, well-rounded. Head rather narrow, ears medium-long and erect. Temperament is generally calm.

Giant Rabbit Breeds
(mature weight frequently above 12 pounds).

Checkered Giant: 12+ pounds. White with spots of black or blue on the nose, cheek, back, and hindquarters. It has a racy type body with an arch to the back. The head is relatively large; ears long and erect. Some rabbit owners claim this breed takes extra care because the racier body is more prone to injury, and the large size makes handling difficult. Not for a first-time rabbit owner.

Flemish Giant: 14+ pounds. Massive long body, ears long and upright. Fur is black, blue, fawn, light gray, sandy, steel, or white. This rabbit takes strength to handle.

Blue Flemish Giant. Hermione.

Giant Chinchilla: 12+ pounds. Fur is banded slate-blue,

pearl, and black. Body is long and full, ears long and erect.

other considerations

Age

It is probably best for a first-time rabbit owner to adopt a mature rabbit between one and three years old, and which has already been spayed or neutered. Older rabbits are much easier to house-train and also much less destructive. Very young rabbits will quickly learn to urinate in the litter box, and then forget just as quickly two minutes later while they're sitting in your lap! Another advantage to an older rabbit that has already been spayed or neutered is that you will not have the worry and expense of getting it altered. But if you are one of those who just cannot resist the incredibly cute little tiny bunny (and I've been guilty of it myself), be prepared for more messes, more caretaking time, more training time, and more destruction.

Gender

Either sex of rabbit can make a good pet. Some people claim that does (females) in general are more aloof, but like the claims for typical breed personalities, any individual can prove the generality wrong. I have both males and females, and cannot say I prefer one to the other as a house pet. Remember that does will tend to be slightly larger. Either sex will need to be altered to make the best house pet, as both males and females are likely to spray urine upon reaching sexual maturity. Unaltered rabbits will also leave more territorial droppings and are likely to be more aggressive.

One caution if you do decide to get a young rabbit. Shelter workers, pet shop owners, private owners, and even breeders may not properly sex a very young bunny. It can be difficult for even experienced rabbit handlers to tell the difference with very young rabbits. This may not matter if only one bunny is adopted, but if more than one rabbit is adopted, misidentification of gender could result in an unwanted litter of rabbits. Have your veterinarian verify the sex of your rabbit when you take it in for its first exam.

If You Have Other Pets

A prospective rabbit owner should be aware that special precautions will need to be taken with sanitation in any household with both rabbits and another pet. Dogs, cats, birds, and reptiles all carry organisms that can infect rabbits (see entries under "parasites" and "bacterial diseases," Chapter 12). Rabbits and guinea pigs can also infect each other with various organisms.

If you have a dog or a cat, you may wish to think about getting a slightly larger rabbit. Dwarf rabbits may appear to be nearer prey-size, especially to a cat. If you have a ferret, you may wish to think twice about getting a rabbit unless you are able to keep them in separate rooms. Many rabbits never learn to relax near ferrets. Rabbits and reptiles are simply not a good combination. Reptiles carry salmonella, which can be deadly to rabbits (see "salmonellosis," Chapter 12), and rabbits are normal prey of many of the larger reptiles.

How Many Rabbits?

Starting with a single rabbit is probably the best way for a first-time owner to go. An exception to this might be the owner who will have to leave the rabbit home alone all day while he or she is at work. In this case two rabbits might be better so they will not get too lonely. I would recommend adopting two already-bonded rabbits. Not all rabbits bond, and it can be a lengthy process for those who do bond (see Chapter 8).

Remember too, the more rabbits you have, the more expense and time they require. If you find you love rabbits you can always adopt more in the future. That's what I did—I started with one, and soon had nine.

adopting your rabbit •

Shelters

I strongly recommend adopting your rabbit from a local shelter or rescue group. Nothing feels better than giving a rejected or abandoned pet a second chance at a happy life and seeing it blossom, given love and attention. Some of these rabbits will already be altered, and save you the time, expense, and worry. Not all shelters handle rabbits, however. If you live in an area where this is the case, there are some shelters that allow out-of-town or even out-of-state adoptions. Best Friends Animal Sanctuary in Utah has many adorable rabbits waiting for a good home, as do many local Rabbit Rescue organizations and shelters (see Appendix I).

4-H Clubs

Another place to find rabbits is your local 4-H club. Youths taking rabbit projects learn to raise rabbits for show, pet, and commercial purposes, and will often be willing to sell one of their rabbits to someone who will provide a good home. If the 4-H program is a well-taught one, the youths taking it learn proper handling, grooming, nutrition, and other facts about rabbits and will be happy to share their knowledge with you.

County or State Fairs

An excellent place to see lots of different breeds of rabbits and talk to their owners is the county or state fair. You will be able to see what the rabbits look like, how big they get, and can talk to people who own that breed. It was at a fair that I first learned about the beautiful changing colors of the Champagne D'Argent and felt the velvet-like fur of a rex. Many of the rabbits at fairs are for sale, and the choice is much wider than most other places you will find rabbits.

Rabbit Breeders

You can also obtain a pet rabbit from a breeder. While there are many horror stories about uncaring breeders who raise their rabbits in miserable, unhealthy conditions, there are many reputable breeders as well. Reputable breeders keep their rabbits in good health and do not raise more than they have a ready market for. Most breeders care enough about their rabbits to feed and house them properly, some give all their rabbits toys, treats, and daily attention, and a few care deeply for their rabbits and mourn each one they lose.

If a breeder is your choice I recommend asking to see the breeder's facilities first. A reputable breeder who cares for his or her rabbits will be glad to show you around and will be able to provide good tips on handling, feeding, and caring for your rabbit. If a breeder doesn't wish you to see the facilities, beware! Don't get your rabbit there.

Pet Store

A final option is a pet store. Rabbits at a pet store can be more expensive and may not be healthy. Moreover, employees are frequently unable to sex rabbits properly, and may give misinformation on the breed and how big it gets. I met one person who had been told she was buying an adult Mini Lop (adult weight about 4½–6½ pounds.) and was dismayed when the rabbit turned out to be a young French Lop (adult weight 10–14 pounds.).

However, just as there are reputable breeders, there are reputable pet store owners. A pet store owner who cares about the animals he sells will not encourage impulse rabbit adoptions, especially at Easter. The owner should ask you how much experience you have with rabbits, and if you don't have any, he or she should recommend you purchase books about rabbits and educate yourself about them before buying one. Be very cautious about buying a rabbit at any pet store where the employees appear more anxious to make a sale than to inform you about the special challenges of having a pet rabbit.

What to Look For

When you do find a rabbit you like, there are a few things to look for that indicate good health. The rabbit should be bright-eyed, not have excessive nasal or eye discharge, and the coat should be shiny and healthy looking. It should be alert, lively, and react to noises. If the rabbit passes these first tests, turn it upside down and check to be sure there are no feces matted on the hindquarters or bald spots on the bottoms of the hind feet. Finally check the teeth for any malocclusion. The incisors should align properly and the teeth should not protrude from the mouth.

Wherever you get your rabbit, insist on a small supply of the pellets the rabbit has been eating. Rabbits are very sensitive to changes in their food and you will need to mix the pellet the rabbit is used to in with the one you have purchased to prevent gastrointestinal problems.

Adopting Special Needs Rabbits

Although it can be difficult for some of us to leave an older rabbit or one with physical or behavioral problems behind in a shelter, I don't recommend adopting such a bunny until you have some experience with rabbits. Caring for special needs rabbits takes a great deal of time and skill, and although it can be rewarding, heartbreak is often part of the package. Raise a healthy rabbit first, and then take on a special needs rabbit if there is room in your heart and home.

One exception to this could be a rabbit with a minor problem. One year at a county fair I saw two beautiful big black rabbits in cages in the back of the building. They were healthy looking, with bright eyes and shiny coats, alert and responsive, but they both had only one ear! The mother had completely chewed off one ear on each rabbit. (This can happen with rabbits, particularly with first-time mothers.) The boy whose rabbits they were had brought them to the fair hoping to find homes for them despite their odd appearance. A rabbit like this would not require a great deal of extra time or care, yet such rabbits have a more difficult time finding homes because of their appearance. (At the end of the fair I asked about the rabbits, planning to adopt one if they were still there, but they were gone and as far as the building superintendent knew they had been adopted.)

Some lop-eared rabbits are born with a condition called "helicopter ears" in which the ears neither stand up nor lop completely. These rabbits may also have a more difficult time finding homes because of their appearance, but the ears are unlikely to cause any serious care problems. So think about adopting one of these rabbits with a minor handicap if you haven't had a special needs rabbit before.

And Yet . . .

Chances are that despite all the advice in this chapter and whatever intentions you have when you go to look for a rabbit, in the end your rabbit will probably choose you. You will see that one special rabbit that appeals to you, and he or she may not be at all the breed, sex, or age you planned on! This has happened to me more than once— I always preferred the looks of larger, brown, stand-up eared bunnies that reminded me of wild rabbits. Yet three of my nine rabbits are small lop-eared bunnies. I saw them, fell in love with them, and that was that.

before bringing bunny home

before you bring your new rabbit home, it is essential to be prepared. It is a good idea to have a cage, food, and other basic supplies on hand, and to have your house rabbit-proofed. You can keep a rabbit in a cardboard box or other temporary quarters for a short while, but it will be much easier and more comfortable for the rabbit if you have a cage and a few other items ahead of time.

cages, feed, and supplies

Rabbit Cages

Buying the cage ahead of time does mean you will have to have some idea of how big a rabbit you will be getting. The cage needs to be large enough for a litter pan and dishes and still have enough room for the rabbit to stretch out full length. Generally, an 18″×30″ cage is adequate for rabbits under four pounds, 2′×3′ for

A high-sided small mammal cage can work for a smaller rabbit that gets lots of time out for exercise.

rabbits four to eight pounds, 2′ × 4′ for rabbits eight to 12 pounds, and 3′ × 5′ for rabbits 12 pounds or more. If the rabbit is going to be out loose in the house most of the day, the cage can be slightly smaller. A good rabbit cage should preferably have a solid, easy-to-clean floor, a side door which can be left open for the rabbit to hop in and out on his own, and a door or other opening large enough to get a litter box through easily.

Many of the cages made specifically for rabbits are utilitarian models intended more for people who are raising rabbits commercially than for people with pet rabbits. These cages are often made of galvanized steel and have wire floors with a pan for collecting urine and droppings underneath. Although these cages may not be particularly pleasing aesthetically, they have the advantage of being relatively inexpensive and can be easily adapted for house rabbit use. A cardboard or piece of plywood should be placed over half the wire floor so the rabbit has a place to rest where its feet will not be irritated by the wire and so its litter area will be distinct. It is also a good idea to purchase urine guards for the cage. These are bands of galvanized steel which attach to the lower edge of the cage and help keep urine and droppings in the cage. Rabbits often back up to the very edge of a cage or pan to urinate, and if the sides are not high enough urine will get on the wall and floor.

More visually appealing cages made specifically for house rabbits are becoming easier to find, although they are also significantly more expensive than the utilitarian cages described above. These cages are often made of epoxy coated wire available in different colors, and may have high plastic sides and wheels for easy moving. Several companies that sell different kinds of rabbit cages are listed in Appendix I.

It is not necessary to purchase a cage specifically made for a rabbit. Guinea pig cages often make good cages for dwarf rabbits, as can ferret cages. One of my favorite rabbit cages is actually a "cat playpen." Its two-inch-high plastic sides keep the rabbit mess from being scattered, it is high enough to allow my rabbit to stand up, and its shelf is a favorite resting place for my Mini Lop.

Transport cages come in handy for trips to the vet.

Another type of cage you may wish to think about purchasing is a transport cage for taking your rabbit to the vet or on short trips. These galvanized steel cages have from one to three compartments, wire floors over a space for litter, hinged tops, and handles for easy carrying. They are usually quite inexpensive, and come in very handy for emergency trips.

The placement of the cage in your home is also important. A rabbit cage should not be placed too near a source of heat like a radiator, register, or woodstove, nor in a drafty cold spot. Loud noise can stress rabbits, so the cage should not be placed right next to a television or sound system speakers. Smoke can predispose rabbits to respiratory problems, so the cage should not be near a fireplace. If a person in your household smokes, it is best to keep the rabbit in a room where smoking will not be allowed. Rabbits like to be where they can watch the activity of the household, but don't enjoy being in a high traffic area. It is best if you can put the cage in a room where you will eventually be letting the rabbit out to explore so he can be getting used to his new territory.

Litter Boxes

It is a good idea to get at least two litter boxes before your rabbit comes home; one for the cage and one for the room where you will first be letting him out to explore. High-sided litter boxes are best, because rabbits like to kick and push litter out and have a tendency to back way up and urinate over the edge of the pan. Ferret litter pans often work quite well for smaller rabbits, and high-sided cat litter boxes serve for larger rabbits. A few litter pans made specifically for rabbits are available, but these can be more difficult to find, especially for larger rabbits.

Litter

A good litter you can buy in quantity locally may be the most difficult thing to find when preparing for your rabbit. Cat litters with additives are not recommended, nor are self-clumping litters. Either can harm or even kill the rabbit if ingested in large enough quantities, and most rabbits will nibble at their litter. Cedar and pine shavings are not recommended because of the aromatic hydrocarbons (phenols) they release, which may harm a rabbit's respiratory system and liver over time. Exposure to these phenols can also reduce the effectiveness of certain drugs used to treat rabbits. Some people use the corncob beddings sold for birds as litter, but these do not control odor very well, and it has been claimed that corncob could block a rabbit's digestive system if too much were to be consumed.

A plain clay cat litter with no additives will work if your rabbit does not consume the litter or dig in it excessively. Clay litter which is consumed can clog the digestive tract with potentially fatal consequences. If the rabbit is a digger, the dust from clay cat litter can make the rabbit more susceptible to respiratory problems. Litter or beddings made from aspen are safe and relatively inexpensive. Newspaper litters are also usually safe but don't control odor well. Hay can be used as a litter, but it bothers some owners to see their rabbits eating the hay from the litter box. Other rabbit owners swear by peat moss. The best litters are those specifically formulated to be non-toxic for rabbits and other small companion animals, but these are often difficult to find unless you live in a large city, although sometimes feed stores will carry them. These specialty litters can also be ordered from rabbit supply businesses (see Appendix I), but freight costs are often high.

Food and Water Dishes

Heavy crockery dishes make the best rabbit dishes because of rabbits' tendency to fling their dishes around and dump the contents. Throwing dishes is lots of fun, and besides, how can a rabbit find the best bits if he hasn't emptied them all on the floor where he can see? Some plastic dog dishes with wide bases to prevent tipping also work if the plastic is hard enough that the rabbit will not be able to chew it. Water can be provided in either a bowl or a water bottle. For smaller rabbits, a hamster or guinea pig water bottle works well. Water in a bottle may be easier to keep clean, but some rabbits do prefer drinking from bowls or cups.

Feed

Correctly feeding a rabbit can be rather complicated (see Chapter 6), but to start out a good high-protein high-fiber pellet and some hay is enough. Rabbit pellets with 14-18 percent crude protein are adequate, pellets with 18-21 percent crude protein are even better. Pellet mixes with grains and dried fruit are not recommended as a staple for rabbits (although they can be given as an occasional treat) because it is thought the high sugar and calcium content of these mixes may contribute to digestive and kidney and bladder problems. Don't forget to ask for a few cups of whatever pellet the previous caretaker has been feeding the rabbit you adopt. Mix some of your pellet in with the old, gradually adding more of the one you will be using. This will help prevent any digestive upsets from the change in diet. Hay should also be provided for the rabbit. Except for young rabbits or rabbits with calcium deficiency, timothy is better than alfalfa (see Chapter 6). Small sacks of grass hay can often be purchased at a feed store or pet store, and larger quantities can be ordered from rabbit supply businesses (see Appendix I). Hay racks that hang on the sides of a cage can be purchased, or an empty tissue box can be used as an inexpensive but functional hay holder.

Toys

A few toys should be placed in the rabbit's cage. An

enriched environment will keep the rabbit from getting bored and reduce behavior problems. Baby toys made out of hard plastic often make good bunny toys. My Mini Lop's favorite toy is a set of plastic keys on a ring made for a human baby. Some cat and bird toys will function as bunny toys, provided the plastic is hard enough that the rabbit won't be able to chew the toy up and ingest it. Rabbits often particularly like toys that make noise, such as cat and bird toys with bells inside.

It is not necessary to buy toys. There are several items from around the house that can make excellent rabbit toys: the cardboard center from paper towel and toilet paper rolls, hard plastic tops from liquid detergent bottles (well-cleaned), old telephone books (rabbits love to tear these apart), plain brown cardboard boxes, or a tissue box filled with shredded newspaper.

Telephone Number of a Rabbit-Savvy Veterinarian

Finding a good rabbit-knowledgeable veterinarian can be difficult (see Chapter 10), and you should do this *before* bringing your rabbit home.

Vinegar

The last item you should have on hand before bringing your rabbit home is a gallon of white vinegar. White vinegar is excellent for cleaning up accidents inside the cage and out,

Rabbits have to check out everything.

and for cleaning the scale that accumulates in the bottom of the litter box. Strong household cleaners should not be used, as the fumes and/or residue could be toxic to rabbits. White vinegar is also useful for cleaning the rabbit's food and water dishes.

rabbit-proofing

The most difficult part of preparing for your new family member is bunny-proofing your home. Rabbits chew and dig. These are natural behaviors that will not stop because the rabbit is living in your house. There's no way to avoid some destruction of property if you are going to have a rabbit, but you can minimize the damage to both your rabbit and your possessions if you are properly prepared.

To give an idea of the variety of things that pique a rabbit's interest, I've prepared a list of a few of the things that have been chewed on by my rabbits or the rabbits of people I have talked to:

afghan
baseboard
bed frame
books (hardback
   and paperback)*
bookcase
boots
carpet
cat tower
cellular phone
chairs

Christmas tree
Christmas lights
Christmas tree ornaments
Christmas presents
cupboards
curtains
doors of all kinds
doorstops
electric cords*
employment application
floor register covers

flyswatters	shoes*
footstools	shower curtains
gunstock	socks
hairbrush	stairs
luggage	stuffed toys
paper towels	table legs
paintings	table leaves
photographs	throw rugs
picture frames	toilet paper
pillows	trash sacks
placemats	trunks
purses	typewriter
quilts	video tape
remote control buttons*	wallpaper
reports	yarn

items rabbits appear to be particularly determined to chew

Some things you can protect by keeping them out of the way of your rabbit, but others are more difficult. **Electric cords** are undoubtedly the biggest danger. A rabbit can be seriously shocked, burned, or even killed by chewing electric cords, and I have yet to meet a rabbit that did not love to chew electric cords. Some rabbit owners have had success spraying a deterrent such as bitter apple on cords, but in my experience this only works for a day or two, if that. The best solution is to cover the cords. There are several ways this can be done. One is with fish tank airline. It has to be slit lengthwise but has advantage of being clear and less obvious than some of the other coverings. My favorite is the spiral wrap available at some electronics stores for wrapping cables. My rabbits don't chew this as much as other cord coverings, and it is flexible. Automotive stores often stock a black covering that has the advantage of being already split down the middle and which comes in different diameters. The wider diameters can be used to cover several cords at once. There is also a flat-sided cord covering available in white and beige that attaches to the wall. This covering is hard enough that rabbits don't ordinarily chew through it, and it is unobtrusive. However, it is also more expensive and difficult to find.

Remember, covering a cord will not necessarily keep the rabbit from chewing on it. You will need to check the cord coverings periodically for signs of gnawing and add more layers of covering if needed.

Another danger is **cabinet doors.** Rabbits can learn to pull them open with their teeth, bringing them in contact with dangerous cleaners, medications, or other rabbit-toxic items. If your rabbit learns to open cupboard doors, install locks or fasteners that resist the pull of the rabbit's teeth.

Carpet will be another difficult thing to protect. Most rabbits love digging at carpet and pulling the fibers out with their teeth. Unfortunately, in addition to ruining your carpet, they may ingest the fibers and end up with an intestinal blockage. Rabbits will often choose spots behind or under things to dig, such as under beds or behind chairs. I discovered one of my rabbits had been busy behind the floor-length curtains in the living room—he had completely dug up a strip about two inches wide by three feet long before I had any idea what he was doing. I stopped his digging by placing pine four-by-fours along the wall. They didn't show under the draperies, and effectively stopped his digging.

Boards can also be used to cover favorite digging spots under beds or chairs. Some rabbit owners completely box in their beds with boards and then hide the boards with dust ruffles.

Books, another favorite with rabbits, can best be protected by keeping them out of reach. Take books out of the bottom shelves of bookcases, or cover that shelf with Plexiglas. Plexiglas is also good for blocking off the way behind re-frigerators, stoves, washers, and other appliances with dangerous high-voltage electric cords. I attach it to the appliance with white stick-ons and it is not very noticeable. Plexi-glas can also be used to protect **wallpaper.** If a rabbit

Rabbits find bookcases wonderful places to look for things to chew.

finds a loose edge on wallpaper, he is likely to strip off a good section before you realize what he's doing. Covering the wall with Plexiglas from the baseboard up about one foot will usually prevent this.

Furniture can be more difficult to protect. If you have valuable antique furniture and want to have a house rabbit too, the best solution is probably to keep the rooms with the furniture off-limits to the rabbit. I know of no solution that is 100 percent effective in keeping rabbits from damaging furniture. Some people have success with sprays like bitter apple, but I have not found them any more effective on furniture than electric cords. I have had some luck covering rabbit chew spots on furniture with clear packaging tape. It doesn't show too much, and the rabbits seem to dislike chewing through the tape.

Houseplants are another thing to think about when rabbit-proofing your home. Consider getting rid of those which could be harmful to your rabbit, or move them to an off-limits room. Even those plants that won't hurt a rabbit, such as geraniums, may be eaten down until there's not much left, and are probably best moved out of reach. Many of the flowers in flower arrangements may be toxic to rabbits, so keep arrangements out of reach as well. See Appendix II for a list of plants that are potentially harmful to rabbits.

Another thing you will wish to keep out of your rabbit's reach is **cat and dog food,** especially the dry food, which a rabbit might choose to nibble. Eating this food can cause a rabbit severe digestive problems. Keep your other pets' food dishes in a place your rabbit will not be able to reach.

These are just some of the things to do to rabbit-proof your home and lessen the chances that your new bunny will be injured or your valuable first-edition book be destroyed. There will be more to do as you learn your individual rabbit's tastes and inclinations. By the time you've had your rabbit loose in your house a year or so, I guarantee you will be an expert on rabbit-proofing a home.

4

the first days

you purchased a cage and accessories and have your house rabbit-proofed (you think), and all is in readiness. It is time to bring your bunny home. You are feeling a little nervous and uncertain as well as excited. What should you do to make his transition to living in your home easier? And what will he do? You know he probably won't chase string like a cat or play fetch like a dog, but what *will* he do?

introducing your rabbit
to his new home

The main thing to keep in mind when you bring your rabbit home is that rabbits are prey animals, and therefore cautious.

Don't expect your new pet to be instantly affectionate and playful. It will take him or her time to adjust to you and your household and feel safe. New environments make rabbits uneasy. They've never seen this territory before. Where are the safe places to hide? What is the quickest way to get to them? What great dangers lurk behind the big dark object (your entertainment center) or around the corner? Where are the good things to chew? Until your rabbit has answered questions like these to his satisfaction, he will be unable to relax and feel at home.

The First Hours

When you arrive home with your new rabbit, put him in his cage and leave him there for a few hours. You can sit next to the cage and talk to him, but your rabbit needs to learn that the cage is his safe place. If you have other pets, now is not the time for them to meet (see Chapter 8). Let your rabbit become accustomed to the new smells and sounds of your house while in the safety of the cage. Don't overwhelm him if there are several people in your household; allow no more than two in the room with him at a time. After several hours you can open the door and let him come out if he wants. Never force your rabbit out of his cage by reaching in and lifting him out unless it is necessary for medical treatment. If he does come out, let him look around and sniff things.

Your rabbit will probably come over to you of his own accord during his investigations of his new territory. When he does, let him investigate you a minute or so. Then it is OK to pick him up and hold him in your lap a minute or two, gently stroking his head and nose. You will need to be able to handle your rabbit, and it is necessary to touch him and hold him to get him accustomed to you. But if he wants off your lap, let him down immediately. Rabbits dislike being held against their will, and will learn to dislike being in your lap at all if you force them to stay.

Holding Your Rabbit Properly

Practice lifting your rabbit in the correct manner until

you feel comfortable handling him. Rabbit skeletons are relatively fragile, composing only 7–8 percent of their body weight, as compared with 12–13 percent in cats. The combination of a rabbit's fragile skeleton and powerful muscles makes it easy for fractures of the spine to occur. Broken backs are common injuries in pet rabbits. A rabbit's spine may fracture if it twists and kicks in your grasp, if you let its hindquarters dangle unsupported, or if you allow it to jump from your arms when you are standing.

The keys to holding a rabbit correctly are to always support the hindquarters and to hold the rabbit firmly. You can lift smaller rabbits by sliding one hand under the chest, grasping his forelegs between your fingers, and cupping the rabbit's hind-

Some rabbits like to be held, but be prepared to hold on if he tries to leap.

quarters in your other hand. Cradle the rabbit against your chest or tuck the rabbit's head under your arm, supporting his rump with your other hand at all times. You can also turn him so that his feet are against your chest, using one hand to hold his shoulders and the other to support his rump. To release the rabbit, kneel down and set him on the floor or allow him to hop onto the floor from your lap.

To pick up medium-sized rabbits, you can kneel alongside the rabbit, slip your arm over his body, and cup his chest with your hand. Lift the rabbit, using the length of your forearm to help support him as you hold him against your side and chest. Slip your other arm around to give additional support to his hindquarters. Do not rise from the floor until you have a secure hold on your rabbit. If your rabbit is too large to lift this way comfortably, you can approach the rabbit from behind, lift under the rabbit's chest with one arm, and support the hindquarters with the other arm.

If it is ever necessary to take a rabbit out of his cage for medical treatment, take him out back first, one hand under the chest and the other supporting his hindquarters. Never lift any rabbit of any size by his ears or by the scruff (loose skin at his shoulders). These are delicate areas with skin and veins that are easily torn.

Don't forget to hold your rabbit very firmly at all times. A phone ringing, a door slamming, a cough or sneeze, a loud noise on television—any of these things and hundreds of others may cause your rabbit to suddenly spring from your arms with a powerful kick of his hind legs. If you are not prepared for this, the rabbit will go flying and may get hurt. One of my rabbits leaped from my arms and missed striking his head on the corner of a sharp hearthstone by a fraction of an inch. Another of my rabbits kicked loose and hit the carpeted floor with such force that he bit the inside of his lower lip. He later developed an infection in the bite. Remember, rabbits do not stop to look where they are going when frightened, all they think about is getting away. Should you feel your rabbit getting loose, drop immediately to your knees so the rabbit will not have as far to fall.

what to expect as your rabbit settles in

As your rabbit becomes accustomed to you and your home and loses his fear, his true personality will begin to unfold. You will begin to see behaviors that will delight and amuse you (and a few that will exasperate you). But don't expect that your bunny will suddenly turn into a marvelously sweet and cuddly pet that snuggles in your lap every night while you watch television. You might occasionally be the recipient of such behavior, especially if your rabbit is older, but don't count on it.

What *can* you expect? This depends partly on the age of the rabbit you have adopted. Younger rabbits are much more active and destructive than older ones. It also depends on the individual personality of the rabbit. Rabbits have personalities that vary as much as those of cats, dogs, or people. You could have two rabbits of the same sex from the same litter, and one might be an intrepid adventurer while the other might like to cuddle and sit. Generally though, you can expect an insatiably curious, immaculately clean, and wonderfully affection-ate pet that will occasionally delight you with fast-paced bunny antics and surprising behaviors.

Curiosity

The inquisitiveness of rabbits makes the fabled curiosi-ty of cats look tame! Most rabbits will check out every single thing in their territory every day. In the wild their survival depends upon an intimate knowledge of their environment, and the rabbit in your house is no different. He or she needs to know where the safe places, escape routes, and tasty books are, as well as the possible dangers. Any new item in a rabbit's territory, be it a grocery sack, letter, or piece of furniture, will probably be cautiously and thoroughly investigated (and maybe tasted).

One of the most entrancing behaviors of rabbits is when they stand on their hind feet, front paws hanging down, head up and alert, and look around. The rabbit is scanning, checking things out. Rabbits have a wide field of vision (about 190 degrees with each

Any new thing in the house will pique a rabbit's curiosity.

eye), and their eyes quickly detect any motion, although because of the placement of their eyes they do not see well directly in front of their noses. Rabbits will often take a bite of food and then stand up on their hind legs and look around while they chew it, turning their heads to get a full view. You can see this same behavior in wild rabbits.

A rabbit intrigued by something new in his environment but not particularly frightened of it will probably approach it slowly and stretch his neck out, ears pointing forward over his head, nose working rapidly. Lop-eared rabbits will assume the same stretched-neck, ready-to-run stance. Their ears may swing forward a little, depending on how much control they have over them.

Chinning

As rabbits investigate their surroundings, you will see them rubbing their chin over items in a quick forward movement. Male and female rabbits that are not yet altered are particularly zealous in this behavior. Called "chinning," this is a form of territorial marking, and rabbits are very territorial. It is extremely important to them to establish who is who in the social order. Among wild rabbits—and domestic rabbits are far less removed from their wild ancestors than either dogs or cats— the dominant rabbits have first chance at the good food and best burrows, and rabbits at the bottom of the social scale could even starve.

So expect a lot of chinning from your rabbits. Rabbits may mark furniture, food, dishes, cages, or their owners in this manner. At first thought to be primarily a male behavior, researchers discovered it is performed nearly equally by both sexes. Neutering or spaying will reduce the amount of chinning behavior, but will not completely eliminate it. Marking items in his territory makes the rabbit feel comfortable and helps him establish his place in the social order if there are other rabbits in the house. One researcher has suggested that when a rabbit becomes dominant a fixative is added to the secretions from the chin gland, causing that particular rabbit's scent to remain longer than the other rabbits. Chinning does not leave an odor humans can detect, and I have never had it leave a stain on anything.

Running and Leaping

A happy healthy rabbit loves to leap and run. Rabbits can run up to 25 miles per hour (40 kilometers per hour) for short distances, and leap 10 feet (three meters). Sometimes a rabbit will suddenly jump straight up into the air from a crouching position. If he watches you intently while he does this, it could be an invitation for you to do the same, after which he may repeat his jump. I have one rabbit who thinks this is part of the morning routine—he jumps, I jump, he jumps, I jump. Not all rabbits like the jump returned—some may find your jumping frightening. In that case, just admire *his* jumps! Rabbits may also jump and whirl around in the air, landing facing a different direction. One of my rabbits likes to do this every morning. Afterward he always turns his head to look at me and be sure I saw his bunny trick.

Rabbits are runners. In the wild they run to flee from danger, to court another rabbit, to establish or maintain their place in the social order, and sometimes for the sheer joy of it. In your home your rabbit may dash madly down the hallway or tear around in circles in a large room. Some rabbits like to make a game of it—first they chase you, then you chase them. I had one rabbit who would play this chase and switch game until I couldn't run anymore (I didn't know how out of shape I was until I got a rabbit). As with jumping, not all rabbits like it if you join in their game. Try it slowly at first and see how your rabbit reacts. If your chasing him makes him frightened or uncomfortable, confine yourself to being chased by him, or just admire his speed as he tears about your house. Rabbits like to be praised and admired. One of my favorite bunny tricks is when a rabbit runs full speed down a straightaway, leaps suddenly into the air, makes a 180 degree turn, and lands going full speed back the way he just came. This must be an effective trick for escaping predators in the wild!

Don't mix happy running with panic running. A badly frightened rabbit may run in panic back and forth in a room or cage. You can tell it from happy running because a panic-stricken rabbit will crash into walls or furniture. Rabbits frightened to this degree are vulnerable to injury, and it is important to get them to stop. Talk to them in a soothing voice. If you can figure out what incited the panic (a dog running into the room, a vacuum cleaner running), remove or stop the cause. If the rabbit is in a cage, try covering the cage by unfolding a blanket over it (very slowly, talking all the while in a soothing voice so as not to add to his panic).

Dancing

A rabbit dance (sometimes called "binky bunny") is difficult to describe but unmistakable if you see it. The rabbit shakes his head side-to-side while making little hops forward (usually looking right at you) and will sometimes end in a dash in which he kicks his hind feet sideways in the air as though clicking his heels. A rabbit "gone binky" is an extremely happy rabbit, and you will know you are doing things right if you see this behavior! As with other bunny antics, your rabbit may or may not want you to reciprocate. Try imitating binky bunny behavior and watch his reaction (and that of your friends and family).

Pushing and Tossing

In the wild, rabbits use their heads and teeth to move

things when looking for food and making their way through cover. You will see your rabbit move things by pushing with his head, and also by tossing. One of my rabbits is an obsessive licker who loves to jump up with me when I'm lying on my bed reading and lick my face. My eyeglasses get in his way, and he always pulls them off my face. Not satisfied with simply removing them, he tosses them repeatedly until they fall off the bed and onto the floor.

Rabbits may also express frustration or aggression by tossing things. A rabbit who wants out of his cage may start tossing everything in his cage from his water bowl to his litter box. If you respond to this behavior by letting him out, it is guaranteed to continue! A rabbit who sees another rabbit near his cage may also throw things about.

It is amazing what a rabbit can lift and toss with its teeth. One of my rabbits—a tiny runt Dutch—was able to lift a heavy glass water bowl that weighed as much as he did and throw it over. My Mini Lop lifts her entire litter box, filled with heavy wheat pellets, and tosses it several inches. Some owners clip or wire the litter box in place to prevent such spills.

Rabbits will often push things about with their heads. Bigger rabbits may even shove furniture around, especially items such as chairs, stools, and footstools. I once had a rabbit that used this shoving behavior in a unique manner. I was walking past my dining room and saw my Dutch rabbit on the table eating an Easter lily. I wondered how he had jumped so high, and then noticed a box I had carelessly left next to a chair. He had jumped from box, to chair, to table top. I lifted my rabbit off the table and shoved the box away. A while later, he was back on the table eating the lily and the box was back by the chair. Knowing how rabbits shove things, I guessed he had accidentally pushed the box back to the chair and gotten back on the table. This time after I took my rabbit off the table I shoved the box farther away. A few minutes later I walked past the dining room and there he was again chewing on the lily. I repeated this three more times, each time moving the box farther away, and each time he shoved the box back to the chair. The interesting thing was that there were no immediate obstructions in the way of the box when I moved it. The rabbit *could* have pushed the box in any direction, but did not. He only pushed it in the direction of the chair. (I gave up and moved both the box and the lily out of the room.)

Rabbits also like to push and pull things with their feet. Try giving a rabbit a bath towel. He may scrabble at it, shove it with his front feet, and pull it around with his teeth, to all appearances trying to "arrange" it to his satisfaction. Many rabbits will do this with afghans on sofas and blankets on beds. Although it is fun to watch, you'll need to take the towel or afghan away if the rabbit begins to eat it.

Climbing

Rabbit owners are often surprised that some rabbits like to climb on things. Although they will jump onto furniture and other objects when they can, I have seen rabbits reach up with their forepaws and pull themselves up with a limb-by-limb walking motion in places where jumping was difficult. Rabbits like to explore, and can be very determined about finding a way to get somewhere they want to go. Not all rabbits like to jump or climb onto things; some rabbits dislike ever getting above floor level. If your rabbit is one of these, don't force him to get up higher than he wishes.

Chewing

This is probably one of the bunny behaviors you will like least, but rabbits do chew, younger rabbits more than older ones. Rabbits will give most anything an exploratory nibble, but confine serious chewing to things that taste good or have a pleasing texture to them. If you have rabbit-proofed your house well, your property loss will be minimized, but sooner or later your rabbit will start gnawing on something you would rather he didn't, so keep watch. Remember that supplying safe sticks and toys will help reduce destructive chewing.

Digging and Burrowing

Wild rabbits spend a great deal of their time digging and burrowing, and your rabbit will likely try to do this also. It is amusing to watch a rabbit burrow around under the bed covers, but not so funny when he digs a hole in the carpet. Providing your rabbit with a box filled with peat moss or crumpled newspaper to burrow in can help reduce destructive digging. Giving your rabbit something to shred with his claws, such as a telephone book or straw whisk broom, will also help reduce unacceptable digging.

Some rabbit owners like to let their rabbits outside to dig. If you choose to do this, be very careful or you may lose your rabbit. It is best to create a secure space by sinking a wire fence a couple of feet under the ground, laying a wire floor, and then backfilling the space. The top of the digging space should also be covered with wire to prevent your rabbit jumping out or predators getting in.

Resting

After an hour or so of bunny antics, your rabbit will probably get tired and want to rest. Rabbits rest several ways, depending on how secure they feel. Sometimes they may lie with paws and hind feet tucked under their bodies, ears lying back (I call this the inscrutable bunny pose). At other times they may stretch all the way out, front legs and back legs extended straight out as far as they will go. Then there is the "bunny flop" where the rabbit turns his head sideways and then throws his whole body on its side, usually with an audible plop. I have seen wild rabbits do this as well, although they don't remain in that vulnerable position for long! Sometimes a rabbit resting on his side will have his legs extended out stiffly, a couple of inches above the ground. This position may be frightening the first time you see it—the first time I saw a rabbit do this, I was afraid for a couple of seconds that he was dead.

Grooming

Rabbits groom themselves frequently and well, spending even more time at it than cats. Rabbits wash themselves rather like cats, and are especially fun to watch when they wash their ears—they hold an ear down with one paw and scrub it inside and out with the other. Rabbits also spend a lot of time washing each other.

Hiding

Rabbits like cover, and will often feel more secure resting under something. A rabbit will probably choose a particular chair, table, or other piece of furniture as his favorite place to rest under while he keeps an eye on things. Other rabbits prefer to return to their cages to rest. Wild rabbits are often more active in the evening, at night, or in the early morning hours, and some pet rabbits also show little interest in coming out of their cages during the day. One of my rabbits would charge around for about an hour in the morning and then hide

Sitting underneath furniture helps your rabbit feel secure.

under my bed all day. No amount of blandishments could get him out from under the bed during the day, although he might stretch his head out far enough forward to grab a treat. Then every evening about 7 P.M. he would suddenly race down the hallway into the living room where he made three big running circles to announce his presence. "I'm here—it's bunny time!"

Affection

Rabbits are social animals, and will likely seek you out at times for some rabbit affection. Your rabbit may come up to you and bump you with his head once or twice (usually twice) and then stretch his head out and down. This is a request for you to groom (pet) your rabbit and also shows he is dominant (you are grooming him first upon request). If he's feeling generous, he may then lick your hand (or your clothes, or the sofa he is lying on) in return. Most rabbits like being stroked from the top of their head to their rump. Some enjoy this so much they will flatten out into a bunny puddle or rabbit rug. If you stop stroking your rabbit before he wants you to stop, he may bump you again or thrust his head under your hand. If you continue to ignore his request, he may scrabble at you with his paws, or, as a last resort, nip you.

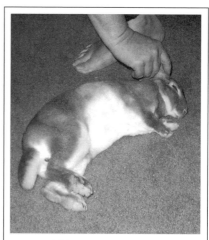

Most rabbits enjoy being scratched behind their ears.

Most rabbits also like having their noses rubbed. (Rabbits generally enjoy being stroked on their face and head because this is where they most often groom each other.) You can do this with your finger, or lie down on the floor and rub your rabbit's nose with your nose. If you do this for a while and then stop, the rabbit may respond by licking your nose a few times and then pushing his nose back under yours for some more rubbing. Some rabbits enjoy having their ears rubbed ever so gently, but be careful not to be too rough, as a rabbit's ears are very delicate. Other rabbits like having their jaws rubbed gently in a circular motion and will grind their teeth in contentment. Few rabbits like to have their underbellies stroked, however, or the underside of their chin. These areas are ticklish and vulnerable.

Making Noise

Although loud or unexpected noises will often stress rabbits, they like to make noise themselves. Rabbits will shake cat toys with bells in them, and they appear to enjoy the noise things make when they throw them. My Mini Lop likes to take her key ring and whap it back and forth on the floor of her cage, making a terrible racket. One woman I spoke to had a rabbit that took beverage cans out of the trash every night and rolled them around on the kitchen floor. They made a wonderful noise and had the added benefit of getting the owner up to play!

5

keeping you and your rabbit happy

there are things that both the rabbit and you will need to have in your relationship to make it a happy one. Some things you will need to train your rabbit to accept, and your rabbit will train you to accept others.

training your rabbit

Litter Training

Probably no single factor contributes more to the owner's happiness than a rabbit that is trained to use a litter box. The ease of this task will depend primarily upon three things—the age of your rabbit, whether or not the rabbit has been altered, and how many rabbits are in your household. Very young rabbits are forgetful, unaltered adult rabbits of both sexes spray urine, and rabbits in multi-rabbit

Babies like these, sweet as they are, will take longer to litter train than older rabbits.

households leave more territorial droppings.

If your rabbit is only 6–8 weeks old, you may as well resign yourself to many "accidents." Researchers have found that younger rabbits require more repetitions to learn a task than do older rabbits. I would certainly agree with this finding from my personal experiences training rabbits!

But if you have succumbed to adopting a sweet little baby bunny, begin the process of litter-training him by noticing which corner of his cage your rabbit tends to use to urinate in. Move the litter box to that corner if it is a different one than where you had placed it. When you let your rabbit out of the cage, I suggest placing him in the room litter box immediately. If he urinates in it, praise him. Continue to place him in the litter box about every five minutes during the time he is out. If you notice him backing up and lifting his tail when he is not in the box, lift him and immediately place him in the litter. Be prepared, however, very young rabbits forget as quickly as they learn. After my first two young rabbits, I noticed that they more or less trained themselves between three and four months of age. My next young rabbits I pretty much left alone except to show them where the boxes were, and they trained themselves too.

It is easier to train the rabbit to urinate in the litter box than to leave all his droppings in it. A rabbit will probably always leave a few scattered territorial droppings (I call them "bunny berries" or "rabbit raisins") around your house. They can be trained to leave the majority of them in their box, however. Rabbits in the wild have "latrines" where they leave most of their droppings. Your house rabbit simply needs to learn his litter box is his latrine. Most rabbits will figure this out on their own, but if yours has difficulty, sweep up his droppings and put them in the box.

For a short time, you will think your rabbit is wonderfully trained, and then between 5 and 7 months of age when he or she reaches sexual maturity, the rabbit will often revert to his previous unacceptable habits, and display a few new ones. Both bucks and does may spray urine if they are not altered. I cannot over-emphasize the importance of spaying and neutering in litter training! The difference between an unaltered rabbit and an altered one can be quite dramatic. My first Dutch rabbit was a case in point. At about 5 months of age, his previous impeccable litter habits simply evaporated. He left bunny berries everywhere (rabbits coat their feces with a secretion from their anal glands that serves to notify other rabbits whose territory is whose), and worse was his new habit of spraying. He never urinated on the floor, but every wall and every piece of furniture was sprayed with urine to about a foot high. And I, his chosen female, was repeatedly doused with urine. I received warm spays of urine in my eyes, nose, and mouth. (Note: do not punish a rabbit for behavior like this or frighten the rabbit by shouting or screaming. It is natural behavior for an unaltered male. More than that, it is actually a sign of affection.) When at six months of age I had him neutered, the difference was astounding. Within a week of his operation he stopped spraying (he never urinated outside his litter box again until his last illness) and began leaving the vast majority of his droppings in his litter boxes.

Training an adult rabbit that has been altered to use a litter box is similar to teaching a young rabbit, but will proceed faster. Show the rabbit where the boxes are and watch to be sure you've placed them in the corners he prefers. Observe him closely the first few times you let him out. If he begins to lift his tail to urinate somewhere other than the box, pick him up, put him in the box, and praise him when he uses it. You may want to leave a little soiled litter in the boxes to begin with in order to show him the purpose of the box. Once your rabbit starts using it on his own, however, the key to keeping his good litter box habit is to keep the litter box clean. Remove the soiled litter once a day, and clean the box thoroughly once a week. Another key to having a rabbit with good litter box habits is to provide enough litter boxes. The more space your rabbit has to roam in, the more boxes you will need to place in strategic corners throughout your house.

However, if you have a multi-rabbit household, as I do, litter training will be more difficult. The more rabbits in your home, the more territorial droppings will be left in places outside the litter boxes. A previously well-trained rabbit may also urinate outside his box upon the introduction of a new rabbit to the household, particularly next to the cage of the newcomer. This behavior can be reduced by properly introducing new rabbits (see Chapter 8), and it will also lessen with time as the rabbits become accustomed to each other. Urinating outside the box will probably stop completely as the rabbits get used to each other, but rabbits in a multi-rabbit household will probably always leave more territorial droppings.

Rabbits eliminate a special kind of droppings a few hours after they eat (see Chapter 6). Called "night" droppings because people rarely see them and because it used to be thought they were eliminated primarily during the night, they are soft, smelly droppings often in a grape-like cluster. In order to obtain needed nutrients, rabbits consume the majority of their night droppings, a behavior called coprophagy. This may seem gross to humans, and we may grimace and say "Yuck!" if we see our rabbits eating them. Please, do not attempt to stop your rabbit from consuming these droppings or punish him for it. Rabbits must eat these droppings to remain healthy.

Discipline and Rabbits

Never discipline a rabbit the way you might a cat or a dog. A rabbit that is thumped on the nose or struck with a rolled-up newspaper is likely to become an excessively timid or extremely aggressive rabbit. Rabbits, because they are prey animals, tend to react to discipline as they would an aggressive act, and that reaction is "fight or flight."

So how can you discipline a rabbit? Some people have reported success in teaching rabbits not to do something by emitting a short, sharp "No" or a high screech. The rabbit either dislikes the noise or interprets it as he would a squeak from another rabbit and may stop whatever he is doing. I have found it depends on the individual rabbit whether this technique works. I had one rabbit that became extremely upset when I screeched. But I did have success teaching two other rabbits not to nip me too hard using this method. Try it a couple of times and see. If your rabbit appears to get upset or reacts aggressively, try another method of discipline. Spraying the rabbit with a water bottle is a method recommended by some, but not by others. There is the possibility that water sprayed in the face could cause respiratory or eye problems. The best methods for training rabbits are simply to remove temptation and reward good behavior.

Sometimes, like young children, rabbits learn they are not supposed to do something and do it anyway. Some owners claim that if caught in the act of doing something "wrong," the rabbit will stop momentarily, look at them, perhaps shake its head, and then intentionally go back to doing whatever it was they were not supposed to do. Other rabbits, like dogs or cats, will hear the owner coming and stop what they are doing, but act "guilty." One of my rabbits knew he was not supposed to chew on my geranium, but could not resist. If he heard me coming he would race out of the room and act busy doing something else. I could always tell by his behavior what he had been doing though, and it was easy enough to verify by smelling his geranium-breath.

Frankly I find the most effective way to train rabbits is to remove temptation and to reward good behavior. Praise the rabbit and pet him every time he does what you want him to do. Rabbits love attention and affection and will learn to do the things that elicit them.

Stubbornness

I have found most rabbits to be quite "stubborn," or difficult to sidetrack from something they want to do. If this stubbornness is expressed by a determination to chew holes in the new sofa or covers off books, it can become very exasperating to the owner. However, it is difficult to win a war of wills with a rabbit. It is simpler to change the environment. Move the item if you can, try spraying it with bitter apple or covering it with clear packing tape to make it unpalatable, or block it off with sheets of Plexiglas.

Like most behaviors of domestic rabbits, "stubbornness" is reflected in the behavior of their wild relatives, as I had reason to learn. I went out one morning to find my car would not start. When I opened the hood, I discovered that several inches of various cables and wires had been chewed off. At first I suspected the squirrels who had been storing food in the engine. Until I opened the hood that afternoon to find a cottontail crouched on top of the engine happily munching on wires. Thus began a month-long battle of wills. I moved the car several times; he always found it. I soaked cotton balls in scents that rabbits don't like and placed them on the engine; he threw them out. I stuffed flexible wire screening in the open spaces of the engine to block him from being able to get in; he pawed and pulled it out. So we compromised. I covered all the hoses and wires in my car's engine with cord coverings and let him stay there (although I still don't think it's the healthiest home he could have chosen). He stopped chewing on the covered wires.

Training a Rabbit to a Harness

Rabbits can be taught to walk on a harness, although any rabbit owner who does this must be cautious. If the rabbit is suddenly frightened while out for a walk it may make a sudden leap and get loose or hurt itself. When you first put a harness on a rabbit, put on the harness part only, not the leash. Leave it on the rabbit while he runs around a little and gets accustomed to the feel. Each time leave the harness

Nineteen-pound white Flemish Giant in harness next to eighty-pound Gordon Setter.

on a little longer. Then snap the leash on and walk with your rabbit while he explores. You will always have to follow your rabbit—the rabbit is not going to behave like a dog on a leash and go where *you* want.

Begging and Treats

One thing a rabbit doesn't have to be taught is how to beg. I've never seen a rabbit who didn't instinctively know how to beg, or any other animal who is as affecting as a begging rabbit (not even a puppy, because the rabbit's inability to bark or whine makes the performance even more irresistible). One favorite begging position of rabbits is to stand on their hind legs and push their nose through the wires of its cage. My Mini Lop has this down to a fine art. She stands, front paws and nose pressing through the wires, white chin and underbelly exposed. "Please, please give the poor captive rabbit a treat to make her captivity just a tiny bit more bearable." It is not one whit less affecting given the fact that the door to her cage is wide open during the performance!

What owners have to watch is that they don't succumb to the begging too often and give the rabbit more treats than are good for it. One of Beatrix Potter's rabbits was given so many sweets that it developed a bad infection in its jaw. Treats such as seeds, toast, and crackers should be given in small quantities, and very young rabbits should not have them at all. Although the connection is not absolutely established, it is believed by many that an excess of carbohydrates can lead to digestive problems, and too many high calcium treats may contribute toward the formation of stones in the urinary tract (see Chapter 6). It is best to give the rabbit a treat that is good for it, like a sprig of parsley or a small piece of carrot or apple. However, I don't think it hurts to give a rabbit a small pinch of sunflower seeds or an oyster cracker once in awhile, as long as you can discipline yourself not to do it too often. This is easier said than done, of course, given rabbits' great expertise at begging.

Teaching a Rabbit Tricks

Some rabbits enjoy learning simple tricks. Sandy Crook, author of *Lops as Pets,* tells of teaching rabbits to do simple tricks such as jumping over a stick or pushing a ball back to the owner. I haven't met a rabbit owner yet who doesn't teach his rabbit to stand or walk on its hind legs by holding a treat above its head. (Careful though—if a rabbit feels he is being teased for a treat too long he is likely to snatch it away and scratch or bite in the process.) Two of my rabbits didn't need me to teach them tricks -on their own they began jumping through the hoop hanging from my cat tower. I don't see anything wrong with teaching a rabbit tricks as long as the rabbit appears to enjoy it. If he doesn't, he'll probably just refuse to cooperate anyway. Rabbits' independence of spirit easily rivals that of cats.

creating a rabbit-friendly environment

Cleanliness

The best way to keep a house rabbit healthy is to keep its environment meticulously clean. Remove soiled litter from the boxes every day, give it fresh water and food, sweep out any bunny berries and spilled food, and clean up any soiled spots in the cage with white vinegar. Most rabbits are possessive about their cages (homes) and will prefer you do this when they are not in them. Wait until they are out before starting to clean the cage. Some rabbits will notice what you are doing and come back to supervise. Give the cage, litter pan, and dishes a thorough cleaning once a week, and once every month or two clean everything with a mixture of one part bleach to ten parts water. Strong household cleaners are not appropriate because they contain chemicals that can harm your rabbit.

Cleanliness is even more essential if you have other pets. Dog, cat, and bird feces often have parasites which can infect your rabbits and make them seriously ill (see Chapter 12). If you have a cat and your rabbit uses the cat's litter box (or vice versa), clean the box immediately after the cat defecates in it, and wash your hands afterward. Keep dog messes cleaned up out of your yard. Clean bird cages carefully so that none of the droppings fall on the floor. If you have any of the above pets, always wash your hands before handling your rabbit (a good idea anyway).

Temperature, Humidity, and Pollutants

Rabbits do best at temperatures between 61 and 70 degrees F (16 and 21 degrees C) and humidity of 30–70 percent. Temperatures below 40 degrees F (4 degrees C) are not good for your rabbit, and temperatures above 85 degrees F (29 degrees C) are dangerous. Rabbits are extremely susceptible to heat stroke. If you do not have air conditioning you will need to take precautions if temperatures rise above 80 degrees, especially if the humidity is also high. A few tips for keeping your rabbit cool on hot days: 1) Be sure the rabbit has cool water. Sometimes placing an ice cube or two in the water bowl can help. 2) Wet a towel and drape it over the cage. 3) Fill plastic water bottles or rinsed juice cartons with water and freeze, then place in the bunny's cage. 4) Refrigerate a piece of ceramic tile or marble and put it in the rabbit's cage. 5) Wet your fingers with icy water and gently stroke your rabbit's ears. A rabbit's large ears act as a temperature regulator and just cooling your bunny's ears will help lower his body temperature. 6) Watch your rabbits closely during hot weather. If you see lethargic behavior and rapid breathing or gasps for air, take the rabbit to a vet as soon as possible (see heat exhaustion, Chapter 12).

Rabbit quarters should always be well-ventilated, but with no draft directly on the rabbit. Cigarette smoke, excessive dust, and certain fumes can irritate the lining of your rabbit's respiratory tract, making it more susceptible to bacterial infections. Fumes from some cleaners, stains, varnishes, and similar products can even be lethal. Remove your rabbit from the area before using such products, and don't bring it back until all fumes have been aired out.

Things That Go Bump in the Night

Sudden noises and sudden movements frighten rabbits in the wild and will frighten rabbits in your home. Don't let a large dog bound up to a rabbit and bark, or allow a very young child to run up and screech in delight at the cute bunny. These things can be terrifying to a rabbit. If you must move furniture or other large objects past a rabbit's cage, take the rabbit to another room first, or cover the cage with a blanket.

Sometimes a person will do things without even thinking of their effect on a rabbit. I did this one year at Christmas. I was bringing in my Christmas tree to set it up, and carried it past the rabbit cage. My rabbit went into a panic upon seeing this huge dark unknown object advancing, throwing himself from one side of the cage to another, knocking dishes, their contents, and litter all over. When I realized what I had done I tried to approach his cage to calm him, but this only made him more fearful (I don't think he recognized me in his terror). Afraid that any second he was going to seriously injure himself, I thought to take an afghan and unfold it slowly and carefully over his cage from the back. He immediately stopped throwing himself back and forth, but he began thumping and continued the thumping for over an hour. Now when I bring in a Christmas tree I make sure my rabbits are elsewhere.

necessities for rabbits

Grooming

Rabbits should be groomed at least once a week throughout the year, and daily during the times they molt. Rabbits molt one to four times a year, depending upon their breed, the heat, and their environment.

Brushing will hasten the molting process and help keep the rabbit from consuming excessive hair. It is during the times of molting that rabbits are at most risk for consuming chunks of hair that could impede their digestion and cause serious complications. I have found that

A long-haired breed such as this Satin Angora requires daily grooming.

a slicker brush works best to remove the loose fur on my rabbits, but other rabbit owners prefer bristle brushes or fine-toothed metal combs. Depending on the breed and coloring of your rabbit, you may see a "molt line" in his fur which will move slowly along the rabbit's face and back as the molt progresses. This line is very obvious on my agouti Mini Lop, but undetectable on one of my other rabbits.

American Fuzzy Lops, the Angora breeds, Lionheads, and Jersey Woolies will require much more grooming than other rabbits. Daily grooming cannot be skipped or their coats will become seriously tangled and matted. If you live where summers are hot, it is a good idea

83

to trim long hair during the summer to help your rabbit cope with the heat. Trim the hair (called "wool" in many of the long-haired breeds) down to about three fourths of an inch or one inch for the hottest months. You can allow it to grow out to its full beauty during the winter.

House rabbits usually need to have their nails trimmed once a month to once a week depending upon how much they wear down. Rabbits provided with digging boxes will not need to have their nails trimmed as often. A guillotine-style cat nail clipper works well for rabbits. Trim each nail a little at a time, being careful not to cut into the dark vein. If you can't see the vein, cut the nails a fraction of an inch at a time until it no longer feels sharp. If a nail bleeds, don't panic. Put a little styptic powder, flour, cornstarch, or baby powder on the end of the nail and let your rabbit return to its cage where it feels safe.

Rabbits often accumulate some dried mucous at the corners of their eyes. Unless it is excessive, this is nothing to worry about. You can help the rabbit groom itself by gently removing the accumulation with a clean finger or cotton swab.

Never bathe a rabbit. If it gets dirty, try brushing it first, then wiping the fur off with a soft cloth or paper towel dampened in water, then brush with a fine bristle brush. Rabbits chill and develop respiratory infections very easily, and unnecessary baths can lead to serious illness and even death.

Spaying and Neutering

Any unaltered pet rabbit should be spayed or neutered upon reaching sexual maturity. Not only does this prevent litters of unwanted rabbits and reduce behavior problems, but there is also good evidence it may help extend your rabbit's life. Uterine cancer is the most common cancer of rabbits. Although this disease accounted for only about 1–4 percent of the deaths of female rabbits under two years old in some studies, it was found to take the lives of almost 80 percent of female rabbits over five years old in another. (This cancer is especially prevalent in Dutch, Californian, and New Zealand rabbits.) Since many house rabbits live past the age of five, it is certainly a good idea to spay a female rabbit to protect her from this inexorable disease, if for no other reason. Neutering your male rabbit may help protect him from testicular cancer.

Goodies to Chew

Rabbits given safe things to chew on will do less damage to things you don't want them to chew or that could be harmful to them. Willow, aspen, and apple branches from trees which have not been sprayed or treated with systemic pesticides or fungicides are the best. If you don't have access to an unsprayed willow or apple tree, many of the rabbit specialty stores (see Appendix I) sell items made from safe woods. Fresh branches from other trees, such as peaches, plums, and cherry are not safe for rabbits to chew, although it has been claimed that dried twigs from these trees are safe for rabbits. Untreated pine boards (not plywood or particle board) are also safe for your rabbit to chew.

Exercise

Wild rabbits are active mammals. They run and chase to

maintain social order, escape from predators, and actively search for food. It is not natural for a rabbit to remain in a small area all the time, and several problems can develop if rabbits are not allowed enough exercise. Inactive rabbits often become obese, and suffer many of the same consequences —cardiovascular problems, stress on the skeleton and joints, sensitivity to heat—that obese people do. In addition, rabbits that do not exercise develop poor bone density and a lack of muscle tone.

Rabbits can be taken outside, but they should be watched closely.

This last can lead to a slowdown of their gastrointestinal tracts (see Chapters 6 and 12), which is a very dangerous condition for rabbits.

All of the above can easily be avoided by letting your rabbit out to exercise for at least a couple of hours a day. It is also a good idea to provide your rabbit with toys or other items to investigate. Rabbits provided with such enriched environments are more active and curious and won't be as prone to the behavior problems and destructive chewing caused by boredom.

It is not difficult to find things rabbits enjoy playing with. Rabbits particularly like cardboard items: oatmeal cartons with the ends cut out, empty tissue boxes, and cardboard boxes of any size. One of my rabbits' favorite things is a two-story cardboard "castle," which they chase each other through, hide in, and tear apart. Rabbit supply businesses often carry various rabbit-safe toys, many of which are inexpensive (see Appendix I).

If you let your rabbit outside to exercise, watch carefully even if you have a portable exercise pen. There are many potential hazards to rabbits outdoors. Dogs, cats, and coyotes can all be dangers to rabbits in suburban yards. Be aware that many pesticides or fertilizers used on lawns

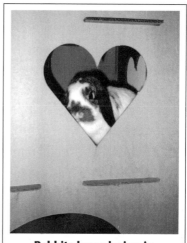

Rabbits love playing in cardboard boxes and special 'castles.'

or gardens may pose a danger to your rabbit if he nibbles on the grass or other plants. Rabbits can burrow out of yards if not watched closely. Finally, rabbits allowed outside may be exposed to disease-carrying insects and other organisms that can cause illness (see Chapter 12).

Routine

Rabbits are animals that like routine and will often get upset if you change things. It is best for the rabbit if you have a specific time each day for letting your rabbit out, cleaning the cage, feeding, and paying attention to him. One rabbit I had was accustomed to getting on the bed each night at nine o'clock, rearranging the bedclothes, and then being petted for 10 to 20 minutes. At 15 minutes before nine he would appear in the living room and wait to be taken to the bedroom. If no one came by 15 minutes after nine, he would begin to show agitation by moving around and putting his ears back. If no one arrived by nine-thirty, he would jump into his cage and refuse to come out for the rest of the evening. Another of my rabbits refuses to come out of his cage at all that day if I do not open his cage within 30 minutes of the usual time. In some cases serious behavior problems can result if a rabbit's routine is changed too abruptly. Make any necessary changes gradually.

Social Interaction

Rabbits are extremely social animals, and need time set aside for you and your family to interact with them every day. A rabbit that is ignored—even if he is let out of his cage and provided with toys—will become isolated, apathetic, and perhaps even ill. Wild rabbits of the same species as our domestic rabbits live in warrens which may have 70 or more other rabbits living in them. A rabbit expects to have frequent social interaction. To a domestic rabbit, your house is his warren, and other animals which live in it, be they cats, dogs, or humans, are his warren-mates. So take the time to give your rabbit love and attention every day. The rewards will far exceed your expectations.

the rabbit's digestive system

the gastrointestinal (GI) tract of a rabbit accounts for between 10 and 20 percent of its total body weight. It is, in the words of Barbara Deeb, one of the contributing authors to the *BSAVA Manual of Rabbit Medicine and Surgery*, "exquisitely complicated and still only partially understood." It is for this reason that rabbit owners must pay so much attention to both what their rabbit eats and what comes out the other end. No other system of the rabbit is affected as quickly as the GI tract when a rabbit is stressed, ill, or has other problems. Unfortunately, it usually takes time and effort to get the intestinal tract working properly again. Too often, the problem is not diagnosed soon enough and in some cases the rabbit dies from complications (see ileus, Chapter 12).

It is not necessary to become a rabbit physiologist, but every rabbit owner should at least understand the basics of a rabbit's digestive system. It really is quite interesting! And since one of the best ways to avoid or minimize digestive troubles and keep a rabbit healthy is to feed it correctly, it pays to learn what foods are good and what foods are bad for a rabbit and why.

ſollowing the track of a rabbit's ſood

Teeth

A rabbit's teeth aren't really that noticeable, yet they are one of the first things a person thinks of when he hears the word "rabbit." A rabbit has three pairs of incisors, one lower and two upper. The second pair of upper incisors is small, unnoticeable, and located behind the first pair. The rabbit's sharp, chisel-edged incisors are open-rooted, as are the molars, and grow continuously throughout the rabbit's life. The growth is quite rapid: rabbit teeth grow about two millimeters a week, or 10 centimeters (four inches) a year (the lower grow faster than the upper). You can see why they must be constantly worn down! If they aren't, a rabbit's upper incisors are likely to curve back, sometimes piercing the palate, and the lower incisors will protrude from the mouth. If uncorrected, the rabbit will eventually die from starvation.

The molars of a rabbit may also overgrow if they are not worn down, but this happens less frequently than it does with the incisors. The lower jaw of a rabbit is much smaller than the upper, and rabbits chew in a side-to-side motion in order to line up the molars and grind their food. They chew rapidly, about 120 times per minute, and this, coupled with the side-to-side movement, gives a chewing rabbit a very amusing appearance.

Stomach, Cecum, and Colon

Once chewed and swallowed, the food goes first into the rabbit's small stomach. From here it passes through a small, muscular opening (pylorus) into the small intestine, and then into the cecum. In the cecum and proximal colon, large insoluble fiber is separated from smaller fiber and soluble carbohydrates and proteins. It is here that the rabbit's digestive system becomes so fascinating. The large insoluble fiber is passed through the colon and out the anal opening as the hard, dry, pellets rabbit owners are most familiar with. But the small fiber and solubles are mixed with a fluid and moved *backward* into the cecum where the mixture ferments. This bacterial action produces volatile fatty acids, K and B-complex vitamins, and bacterial protein. The fatty acids are absorbed by the cecum. The vitamins and bacterial protein remain in the cecal mixture and are passed from the anus some four to eight hours later as the soft, membrane-enclosed "night droppings" (cecotrophs), which the rabbit eats as they emerge from the anus. Unlike the plant matter that the rabbit chews so thoroughly, these cecotrophs are swallowed whole.

This process of eating one's droppings is called coprophagy. The production of these cecotrophs depends upon a delicate balance of beneficial bacteria in the rabbit's cecum; a balance which can be easily upset. Should the rabbit's digestive system slow down due to stress or illness, or be affected by too much sugar or a sudden change in diet, the beneficial bacteria are out-competed by harmful bacteria. The rabbit can become bloated, and the toxins produced by the harmful bacteria accumulate, eventually reaching levels that poison the rabbit.

Some hair in the rabbit's digestive tract is normal. Rabbits consume hair in the process of grooming themselves, and this normally passes through without difficulty. Rabbits do not regurgitate hair as cats do. For a long time, it was thought that rabbits were unable to regurgitate. However, evidence is accumulating that rabbits may in fact vomit, although rarely. Several veterinarians have reported seeing rabbits that had apparently regurgitated and then aspirated food into their trachea and lungs. If regurgitation does occur, it is apparently a rare phenomenon.

The Urinary Tract

Pet rabbits drink about twice as much water (by weight) as they eat food. Water is necessary to moisten the food for processing. Rabbits receiving a large quantity of fresh vegetables in their diets will require less water, and rabbits on high-protein diets will require more.

Rabbit urine is normally colored anywhere along a gradient from pale yellow, dark yellow, orange, brownish, to red. The color comes from pigments in the food a rabbit consumes, or from medications such as antibiotics, and is nothing to worry about. Some new owners worry when they see red urine, thinking it is blood. Blood in the urine is relatively rare in rabbits, and red color is more than likely from pigment. If excretion of red urine continues over three or four days, however, or if the urine is pinkish rather than reddish, you may wish to check with your veterinarian.

You may notice that rabbit urine often has particles in it. These are from calcium. Rabbits (unlike most mammals) excrete calcium in direct proportion to the amount consumed in their diets. Rabbits will normally excrete about 45–60 percent of dietary calcium, compared to about 2 percent in other mammals. Some of this calcium precipitates out in the urinary tract as calcium carbonate, visible as a grainy deposit called "sand." It is

normal for the urine of rabbits to have some of these particles, but a heavy deposit of these particles, or "sludge,"
could indicate a diet too high in calcium or too low in
water. Calcium carbonate crystals may come together to
create "stones" that can cause pain and blockage, so cut
down on high-calcium treats and increase the rabbit's
water if you notice sludge in the urine.

feeding your pet rabbit

The diet of a pet house rabbit should be composed of a
good high-protein pellet, grass, fresh vegetables, an
occasional fruit treat, twigs, and water. Some rabbit caretakers now recommend a pellet-free grass and fresh vegetable diet, but personally I do not think this is necessary. A dried grass and fresh vegetable diet does not truly
mimic a wild rabbit's diet, and in my opinion a small
amount of good-quality high-fiber pellets will not
adversely affect a rabbit's health.

It is interesting that while wild rabbits may end
up eating a high-fiber diet because of what is available,
they do not always select these plants when others are
accessible. Given a choice, wild lagomorphs select high-
protein, low-fiber plants with tender, succulent leaves,
and have a strong taste preference for foods high in sugars. In other words, you cannot count on the rabbit to
eat what is good for him. Like people, rabbits prefer
many food items that are not particularly beneficial to
them in large quantities.

Fiber is the most important thing in a rabbit's

diet. It helps keep the digestive tract moving, passes hair safely through the tract, helps prevent obesity, reduces fur-chewing, and helps maintain the critical balance of bacteria in the cecum. Protein is essential too, although too much protein is *not* good. Diets that are too high in protein put a strain on the kidneys, may lead to an over-production of cecotrophs, and can contribute to a slow-down of the intestinal tract (see ileus, Chapter 12). Growing rabbits and long-haired breeds of rabbits, such as Angoras and the Jersey Wooly, do require higher protein diets in order to maintain their coats, but diets of 14–18 percent protein are adequate for other rabbits.

Large amounts of foods containing sugar and/or fat are never good, although your rabbit will probably let you know he likes them. For a long time it was thought that too much carbohydrate in a rabbit's diet could cause the harmful bacteria in the cecum to proliferate, leading to gastrointestinal problems. It now appears that while this may be true for very young rabbits, older rabbits are better able to digest carbohydrates. Wild rabbits show taste preferences for foods high in sugars, and their diets naturally include plants and parts of plants that are high in carbohydrates. I would suggest you avoid giving young rabbits (under six months) foods high in carbohydrate, but include some in adult rabbits' diets in the form of fruits and grains.

Rabbits need only about 1–2 percent of their daily calories to be from fat, and their systems simply don't handle any more than this very well. Rabbits eating too many fatty foods will become obese and may develop atherosclerosis and fatty liver disease, which are normally rare in rabbits. Obesity is a problem with pet rabbits, and difficult to correct because rabbits cannot be put on diets in the manner of cats or dogs.

While many rabbit books will warn about the dangers of too much calcium in a rabbit's diet, remember that some calcium is necessary. It is essential for strong bones and good dental health. If the rabbit is not showing signs of too much calcium in the diet, i.e. a heavy deposit of sludge in the urine, it does not hurt to give the rabbit a few high-calcium bunny treats. Some good high-calcium rabbit foods include carrot tops, alfalfa, mustard greens, and dandelions. Oats, sunflower seeds, barley, and bananas are good occasional low-calcium bunny treats.

Pellets

A pellet should contain at least 14–18 percent crude protein, 20–25 percent crude fiber, and about 2 percent fat. This comes close to the composition of many grasses. Pellets containing 20 percent or more protein (for growing rabbits and wool breeds) can be special-ordered from some pet and rabbit supply stores. An alfalfa-based pellet is acceptable provided the rabbit is not also fed alfalfa hay, and provided the rabbit does not show any signs of excess calcium in the urinary tract (creamy urine, sludge in urine). There are many timothy-based pellets available from rabbit supply businesses (see Appendix I).

Always store your pellets in a sealed container located in a cool, dry, place. If there is ever any sign that rodents, birds, or raccoons have contaminated the pellets, destroy them. Pellets can also become contaminated with fungi if they are exposed to moisture, and the fungi produce mycotoxins that can be deadly to rabbits.

If you notice that your pellets have become damp, or look like they have discolored, dispose of them.

It happens sometimes that pellets were made from feed already contaminated with mycotoxins, and occasionally pellets have been contaminated with antibiotics such as lincomycin and penicillin, which are toxic to rabbits. Unfortunately, it is difficult for the consumer to tell if this is the case by looking at the pellet. Should your rabbit refuse to eat a pellet he has always eaten before, or consume less of it while he consumes other foods as before, you might consider disposing of the remainder of that sack of pellets.

Rabbits under six months of age can be allowed unrestricted access to pellets. Rabbits from six months to a year can have about ⅓ cup per day per five to six pounds of rabbit. Rabbits one year and older should only have ¼ cup per day per five to six pounds. (For Angora rabbits and Jersey Woolies, increase these amounts to ½ and ⅓, respectively). If you ever change your brand of pellet, do so slowly. A sudden change in diet can up-set the sensitive digestive system of a rabbit, and some rabbits will refuse to eat new pellets unless they are introduced gradually. Always give grass hay and fresh vegetables in addition to the pellets.

Three rabbits enjoying a special basket of healthy treats.

Alfalfa and Grass Hays

Good grass hay is essential in your rabbit's diet. It provides the fiber to keep the gastrointestinal tract moving, helps move hair through safely, improves dental health, and helps prevent obesity. Alfalfa hay is probably what you will find at a pet store, but it is very high in protein, oxalates (oxalates bind with calcium and affect its absorption), calories, and calcium, and is not recommended as a staple for rabbits over one year old, although they can have a little as an occasional treat. Timothy hays are most highly recommended by rabbit care experts. Some rabbits enjoy a little oat hay mixed in. Timothy and oat hays are available from a few pet stores and most rabbit supply houses. "First cutting" hay will be coarser with more stems, "second cutting" hay will be greener and have more leaves. First cutting hay is better for your rabbit, but if your rabbit is a finicky eater and refuses to eat anything but second cutting hay, it is certainly better than no hay. Rabbits of all ages can be allowed unlimited access to grass hay.

As with the pellets, grass must be stored in a cool, dry place safe from rodents, birds, and raccoons. The hay should be green, dry, and sweet-smelling. If you notice any other plants mixed in with the hay, take them out and dispose of them. It has happened that hay has been sold with milkweed and other plants poisonous to rabbits mixed in. The grass should be dry. If it gets any moisture on it and shows signs of fungal growth (mold) dispose of it at once. Grass, like pellets, may occasionally be purchased already contaminated by fungi. Any grass that has yellowish or blackish discoloration should be thrown out.

Fresh Vegetables

Fresh vegetables are another essential in your rabbit's diet. They provide nutrients not found in the pellets and hay, and help the digestive tract to function as it should. Only top-quality vegetables should be given to your rabbit— never give a rabbit rejects from your refrigerator that are starting to spoil. This is a sure way to give your rabbit a terrible digestive upset. All vegetables given to your rabbit should be washed as you would wash them for yourself, and then dried with a paper towel. Rabbits

Rabbits rarely fight over food, but will shove, push, and pull to get it away from each other.

should be fed a variety of vegetables, but always introduce a rabbit to a new vegetable slowly. Give the rabbit a small amount of the new vegetable by itself once or twice and watch for any digestion problems before adding it to your rabbit's diet in combination with other vegetables.

Some vegetables are better for your rabbit than others. The following vegetables can be fed to your rabbit fairly frequently: carrot tops, parsley, cilantro, endive, leaf and romaine lettuce, dandelion greens, flat pea pods, beet greens, and Swiss chard. Vegetables that are not good for rabbits in large amounts but can be given to them as occasional treats include carrots, celery (cut into small pieces), white clover, parsnips, spinach (high in oxalates), mustard greens, kale, peas, and zucchini.

Lists of vegetables that should be given to rabbits only rarely and in very small quantities will vary. My list is perhaps more extensive than many because I think it is better to be more cautious than less: broccoli, cauliflower, cabbage, brussels sprouts, red clover, iceberg lettuce, turnips, and rutabaga.

Some vegetables should *never* be given to rabbits: rhubarb leaves, raw beans, raw potatoes, onions, and sweet corn.

It is not recommended that fresh vegetables be given to rabbits under three months old, as rabbits this young may develop diarrhea from eating too many fresh vegetables. Three to six month-old rabbits can be slowly introduced to fresh vegetables (always one by one so you can monitor the rabbit's reaction to each vegetable). Start with just a bite or two and gradually work up to about a half cup per day by age six months. Keep increasing the amount of fresh vegetables over the next few months until you are giving your rabbit between one and two cups a day for each five pounds of rabbit. Long-haired rabbits can be given a cup more than this.

Don't *over*feed your rabbit fresh vegetables. Rabbits that eat too many can develop intestinal gas, which can be a serious problem for a rabbit (see bloat, Chapter 12). It may be caused by the kind of vegetable or the speed at which the rabbit eats it. You will find that rabbits are usually rather voracious eaters, but it is thought that eating *too* fast—more likely when the rabbit prefers the food—may contribute toward intestinal gas. And remember, only give your rabbit the best quality fresh vegetables. Don't give him old vegetables to clear out the refrigerator.

Fruit

Rabbits often dearly love fruit, and it is a good treat to give a healthy rabbit. They can safely have the equivalent of a couple of tablespoons a day per five pounds body weight for an adult rabbit. Fruits are best not given to rabbits under 6 months old, because the high sugar content may cause an imbalance of cecal bacteria and lead to diarrhea.

Fruits safe for rabbits to eat include apples, peaches, pears, strawberries, blueberries, blackberries, bananas, papayas, mango, raisins, grapes, kiwi fruit, and melons. Rabbits also like fruit juice—I caught one of my rabbits happily lapping up a glass of cranberry juice—but don't allow them to have more than a tablespoon or so, and then only if it does not have added sugar.

Grains

Many rabbits enjoy a treat of grains such as rolled oats, whole oats, or barley. Grains are high-carbohydrate and should not be given to very young rabbits because they can cause an imbalance of cecal bacteria. Do not give a rabbit any grains until he is five or six months old. Rabbits this age and older can safely have about a tablespoon of grain per day.

Twigs

I recommend giving rabbits a few twigs (one-quarter inch or more in diameter) from unfertilized, unsprayed trees as a regular part of their diets. Chewing on them is excellent for rabbit teeth and the bark they consume provides roughage. Apple, aspen, and willow are the best. Not everyone has access to fresh untreated apple, aspen, or willow twigs, however. For those who don't, many of the specialty rabbit supply businesses sell either bunny-safe dried twigs or items made of safe willow such as baskets, tunnels, and chew rings.

Infrequent Treats

I am going to state something that may be a little unusual for a caretaker of rabbits. That is, I do not think it hurts to give an otherwise healthy adult rabbit that is not overweight an occasional treat that is not considered particularly good for it. In this category I would include oyster crackers, toast and bread, alfalfa cubes, peanuts, and commercial seed treats. Or you can buy specially made "healthy treats" from some rabbit supply businesses. Rabbits learn to recognize when they are being given a special treat, and it can boost their spirits when they're a little stressed from a change in your household or the presence of a new rabbit. Special treats also come in handy after surgeries, when it can be difficult to persuade the rabbit to eat anything at all and you are desperate to get *something* into its stomach. So give your rabbit that occasional treat—just don't give in to begging and make it a constant habit.

Feed Times

Wild rabbits usually forage for food in the evening, during the night, and in early morning. Pet rabbits should be given about half of their daily food allotments in the early morning, and the other half in the evening. It is better to split the amounts of each food into half for each feeding so that the rabbit receives both pellets and vegetables morning and evening, although this is not absolutely necessary. You could give pellets in the morning and fresh vegetables in the evening, or vice versa. Grass hay should be available to the rabbit at all times.

Overweight Rabbits

It can be difficult to adjust a rabbit's diet so that it loses weight, which is one of the reasons rabbit owners should be careful not to let their rabbit become overweight to begin with. The amount of food a rabbit receives should never be too drastically reduced, because this can lead to intestinal motility problems. Rather, the *kind* of food the rabbit receives should be changed. Either change to a pellet specifically for overweight rabbits or cut down on the amount of pellets the rabbit is given until it is only ⅛ cup a day given as a tablespoon in the morning and one in the evening. Allow unlimited grass hay. Fresh vegetables can be given, but avoid high-sugar vegetables such as carrots and peas. Fruit should only be given as a rare treat, and grains avoided. Be sure the overweight rabbit receives plenty of time out for exercise.

7

communicating with your rabbit

perhaps nothing is as fascinating to the new rabbit owner as learning how well these "silent" animals are able to communicate. They can't bark, meow, or purr, but you will know nevertheless when they want attention, when there is something to fear, and when they are happy or unhappy. If you don't understand one way they attempt to communicate, they will try another. One thing I have noticed about rabbits is that they are not particularly patient animals. When they want something, they want it *now*. If they don't get it, their rabbit language will become more and more emphatic until they do.

Rabbits communicate with a variety of noises, body language, and the use of other items. One of the primary ways rabbits communicate among themselves is by scent. Every rabbit has his own scent profile by which other rabbits recognize him. It is scent that enables a rabbit to establish his territory and his place in the social order. Rabbits have three kinds of scent glands; chin, anal, and inguinal (located either side of the genitals), the secretions of which differ in their chemical composition. The rabbits use chin and anal glands to mark territory, and the scent from the inguinal glands allows rabbits to identify individuals in the group.

You will not be able to detect the scents rabbits

produce, however, and will have to learn to communicate with your rabbit in other ways. The few noises they make you will learn to recognize the meaning of quickly. More difficult will be to learn to watch how the rabbit's body and ears are positioned and what meaning these postures have. Most entertaining will be the times your rabbit uses a tool to communicate.

ear carriage and body posture

Cowering—Rabbit presses itself to the ground with its ears tightly pressed against its back, eyes bulging. This is a fear position. The nictitating membranes (third eyelids) may cover part of the eye.

Flattening—Rabbit rug or bunny puddle. Rabbit flattens itself against the ground, body relaxed, no sign of tension. Rabbits do this sometimes in response to being stroked. Other rabbit owners have reported their rabbits assume this position when they want attention.

Mandolin rabbit—Rabbit stretches head out toward you (or another rabbit) and lowers it to the ground. Body is usually relaxed with hind feet tucked under. This is a request to be groomed (petted).

Inscrutable bunny—Rabbit lies with hind feet and forefeet tucked under body, ears back but not pressed tightly against back, eyes half-closed or fully closed. This is a common pose for sleeping and also for relaxing while the rabbit keeps an eye on what is going on around him.

Relaxed rabbit—As in above but with front paws visibly extended out from chest. Another pose for watching the world go by.

Totally relaxed rabbit— Rabbit stretches out with both front and back feet extended straight out from the body. Head may be raised or chin may rest between forelegs.

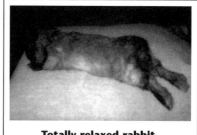

Totally relaxed rabbit.

Rabbit flop—Rabbit turns head sideways and then flops body over on side. He may remain in this position or roll. A rabbit that does this is relaxed and happy.

Half-listening—Rabbit moves one ear up or turns it with the inner part facing the direction the noise is coming from. Rabbit may do this in any pose, but you will probably notice it more often when it is in the relaxed rabbit or inscrutable bunny poses. Lop rabbits usually move one ear forward in the direction of the noise.

Alert rabbit—Eyes wide open, nose wiggling rapidly, ears both up and moving toward the direction of a noise. Rabbits may do this in any pose, but like the above it is more noticeable when the rabbit starts in the relaxed rabbit or inscrutable bunny poses. Lop rabbits have the same open eyes and wiggling noses, but the ears will only swing one way or the other as the rabbit focuses on the noise.

Explorer rabbit—Rabbit is up on his feet, neck stretched out, ears pointing forward over his head. Tail is stretched out straight behind. Nose usually wriggling very rapidly. Rabbit has seen something new that interests it and is checking it out. Lops stretch their necks out and their ears swing slightly forward.

Meeting new people—Pose like above, but ears are only pointed slightly forward over the head and held out in a slight "V." Rabbits meeting a cat or another rabbit will often assume this pose and may come close to touching noses. I even photographed a wild cottontail rabbit and jackrabbit (hare) display this same behavior upon meeting. In Lops it is difficult to tell this pose from the explorer rabbit.

Two lops meeting for the first time. Note the forward swing of the ears.

Periscope bunny—Rabbit stands on hind legs, front paws usually hanging down, and turns his head to look around. Rabbits in the wild do this to be able to see above the tall grass, or to reach a tasty twig.

Attack rabbit—Rabbit is up on feet with legs and

body visibly tensed, tail straight up like a flag, and ears down and back. Head is forward with teeth sometimes visible. This rabbit is prepared for "flight or fight." A rabbit in this position may suddenly lunge forward and bite, so beware!

communicating by touch and with noise

Light nudge or bump with head—A rabbit will often come up and bump a person's leg, arm, or hand with his forehead, usually twice. This is a sign the rabbit wants to say hello or desires attention. If he then puts his head down flat with outstretched neck (see mandolin rabbit) it is a sign that he, the dominant rabbit, wants to be petted. A rabbit that pushes his head under the chin of another rabbit is asking to be groomed by that rabbit.

Shove with head—If you were petting the rabbit and stopped, the rabbit is probably trying to communicate that he wants more. If you are in the act of petting your rabbit when he does this, it is a sign he has had enough.

Head shake—Rabbits often give quick head shakes while running and playing, and it appears to have a playful, happy connotation. Some rabbits give a head shake in response to a reprimand or upon being caught doing something "wrong," at which times there seems to be a little defiance mixed in with the playfulness!

Chinning—Rabbit swipes chin over object or animal in a quick motion. This is a means of marking his territory.

Licking—This is a sign of affection.

Chinning.
Rabbits constantly mark items new and old in this manner.

Lunging—A rabbit that is irritated, angry, or frightened may lunge forward, often striking with his two front feet. The lunge may be accompanied by a spitting noise. Rabbits who are being teased will often respond with a lunge and spit.

Licking is often a sign of affection.

Spitting—One of the sounds a rabbit makes is the spit, sometimes called a hiss or a growl. It sounds something like a cross between a hiss and a growl. As with the lunge, a rabbit that does this is annoyed, angry, or frightened.

Squeak—A high-pitched sound that may occur singly or in succession. It may indicate your rabbit is hurt (I have heard it from a rabbit when bitten by another), or that he is afraid or nervous.

Scream—A sound you hope never to hear, it is made when a rabbit is terribly frightened, in severe pain, or dying.

Nipping—Rabbits in their warren communicate with bites or nips, and so will your rabbit.

A rabbit will often give a sharp nip if it wants attention and you have failed to notice earlier signals, or if you are doing something it doesn't like, such as holding it against its will.

Paw scraping—A dominant, unneutered male rabbit will scrape the ground with his paws upon the approach of another male rabbit. If the other rabbit leaves, all is well. If he does not, the dominant male will likely attack.

Scrabbling—Similar to the above but done in different contexts. House rabbits will often scrabble their paws at your clothes if you have stopped petting them and they want more, if they desire attention, or just for the fun of it. They will also scrabble at loose pieces of fabric, such as towels, blankets, afghans, and pieces of clothing.

Tooth grinding—Rabbit moves his jaws back and forth, producing a soft grinding sound. This soft "purr" is made by a contented rabbit. Rabbits being stroked often make this sound. Some rabbits move their jaws back and forth, but produce no audible noise.

Tooth gnashing—This is much louder than the previous sound, and is a sign of a rabbit in great pain or distress. If you ever hear your rabbit doing this, find the cause or take it to a vet.

Snort—Sometimes called a sniff. Rabbits making this sound appear to be annoyed or irritated. Some rabbit owners report their rabbits do this when presented with a food they don't like. My rabbits do this when I have done something they dislike.

Humming—This is also called grunting, honking, and oinking, which gives an idea how difficult it is to describe this sound. It is usually made by unneutered males in courtship, although you will occasionally hear it from other rabbits as well. Three of my rabbits (two males and one female) make this sound when they are running around the room having a good time. It almost appears to have the same connotation as tooth grinding, that is, of contentment or happiness.

Circling—A courtship behavior. Male rabbits circle their chosen females. If an unneutered buck circles your feet, you may be his chosen mate. Rabbits are able to distinguish gender in humans, and women in particular may be shown quite obvious signs of affection by unneutered male rabbits. This behavior is also seen in neutered rabbits, however. With neutered rabbits it appears to have the connotation "I love you," or "I'm glad to see you."

Thumping—Thumping is primarily an expression of fear, and has been assumed to serve as a warning of danger to other rabbits. A house rabbit that begins to thump might have seen a raven or airplane passing by the window, or heard an unfamiliar noise. House rabbits also learn to thump to communicate things other than fear. Some rabbits will thump in anger if they are put into their cages before they wish. One of William Cowper's hares learned to drum on the poet's knee when he wanted to go out in the garden, and if he was not immediately taken there he would grab Cowper's coat between his teeth and pull.

One of my rabbits learned to thump for attention. One night he began to thump loudly, but I could neither see nor hear anything that might have frightened him. Then I noticed he was staring at me fixedly from the shelf in his cage. When he saw I had noticed him he slowly raised his hind foot and slammed it on the shelf. I realized he was saying "Pay attention to me." Thump. "Now." Thump. "Right now."

other communications

Throwing things—A rabbit that throws things may begin to do so for the fun of it and then learn he can get something he wants that way and use the behavior as a means of communication. Many house rabbits learn that if they make enough noise throwing things they are likely to be let out of their cages. My rabbit that whaps his key ring on the cage floor for attention will throw the ring of keys into his food or water dish if it gets empty. He does not throw them into dishes that still have food or water in them. One day when I was inexcusably late attending to him, I opened his door and said, "Muffy want to come out?" Every other day I had done this he would jump out of the cage immediately. This day he turned his back on me, hopped to the back of his cage, and pushed his water dish to the edge of the door. It was empty except for the key ring. I cleaned and filled it at once and returned it to the cage where he immediately took a long drink. How is that for communicating?

Rattling cage bars—Rabbits may first do this in an attempt to find a way out of their cages. Then they learn that if they rattle the bars of their cages, the owner comes running and lets them out. Soon they have their owner trained to let them out on demand. Other rabbits will shake their cage bars in anger if another (subordinate) rabbit gets too close to the cage.

Rattling toys—One of my rabbits picks up a cat toy with a bell in it and shakes the toy so that the bell rings whenever another rabbit approaches his cage. I have not seen this behavior in him at any other time. Another of my rabbits shakes a belled bird toy when he wants out of his cage. This behavior differs from throwing a toy because the rabbit does not let the object go, but shakes it back and forth while holding on to it.

bunny etiquette

One of the interesting things about rabbits is that they often appear to have a rather strict "etiquette" and will exhibit aggression if you ignore it. Of course, wild rabbits living in a warren have specific things they do and specific responses that are acceptable from the rabbits elsewhere on the social scale. In the home we are their warren-mates, so this behavior is not that surprising. One particular thing I have noticed is that many rabbits do not like to have someone walk close by without acknowledging their presence by a pat on the head or some other sign. One of my rabbits became so upset if I failed to acknowledge his dominant presence when I walked by that he would lunge at me and spit. Then he would turn his back on me and have nothing to do with me for the rest of the day. So ignore your rabbits' communications at your own peril!

behavior puzzles and problems

even the best-cared-for bunny may suddenly exhibit behavior that is confusing or frustrating to the owner. In the following pages I have listed some of the most common behavior problems that arise with rabbits, along with a few tips on how to resolve the situation so that the rabbit, you, and everyone else is happy again.

rabbit-people issues

Inappropriate Elimination

Nothing is more frustrating or inexplicable (to the owner) than when a perfectly litter-trained rabbit suddenly begins to eliminate outside his litter boxes. Fortunately, the reason for this behavior can usually be tracked down and the rabbit re-trained.

The first thing to determine is whether there is a medical reason for the behavior. Is the rabbit dribbling rather than leaving puddles? This may be caused by a bladder infection. Check the urine. Is it pinkish rather than the common reddish pigment? If so, take the rabbit to a veterinarian. Is the urine creamy-looking with sludge, that is, a grainy deposit, in the urine? If so, the problem may be that the rabbit is receiving too much calcium in his diet and is developing a condition that can lead to stones in the urinary tract. This condition may often cause a rabbit to urinate outside his box. See Chapters 6 and 12 for more information. If it is feces the rabbit is leaving where he did not used to leave it, check it also. Is it unusually soft or runny, or does it have blood or mucous in it? If it is either of these you should take the rabbit to a veterinarian immediately. Diarrhea may occur as a result of a diet change, bad diet, or a disease (see Chapters 6 and 12).

If you can see no signs of a medical problem, it is time to look for another reason for his behavior. Did he get frightened while in his litter box one day? Rabbits sometimes avoid returning to places where they received a fright. If this is the case you may need to relocate the litter box. Have you moved the rabbit's litter box, his cage, or other things in a room? Rabbits, being the creatures of habit that they are, usually hate to have their things moved, and may show disapproval by urinating and/or leaving feces outside the box. Have you brought something new into the room? One of my rabbits, who used his box religiously the rest of the year, started urinating on the floor when the Christmas tree was brought into the house. He stopped when it was taken out.

Sometimes rabbits simply decide they want their litter box moved to a different place. Or want a different litter box. Three of my rabbits in a large cage began to urinate on the floor rather than in their litter box. I moved the box to cover the area where they had been urinating on the floor, but they simply began urinating elsewhere in the cage. Puzzled, I tried a different litter.

Still they refused to use the box. Finally I changed the box, putting in a larger one with lower sides. Success! For whatever bunny reason, they had decided they would no longer use the litter box they had been perfectly happy with for the previous ten months.

Another reason for eliminating outside his usual places can be a change in the amount of attention you are giving your rabbit. Have you reduced the amount of time you play with your rabbit? Is it a busy time of year when you might be spending less time with him without realizing it? Giving him extra attention may solve the problem in either of these cases. Do you have a new pet or a new person living in your home? Your rabbit may feel threatened or feel it necessary to make it clear who was there first and is top rabbit. Giving your rabbit extra attention and reassuring him that his place in your affections has not changed may help. Frequently, if a new pet or person in the household is the cause, the inappropriate elimination will often stop after a short period of time when the rabbit feels he has made his point or has become accustomed to the new animal. This is especially common if the newcomer is another rabbit. Rabbits in the wild show discomfort when they sniff the markings and droppings of a strange rabbit, and yours is no different. The rabbit that was in your home first will feel the need to leave extra signs of his presence around until the dominance issue is sorted out.

Perhaps the most frustrating situation is when none of the above applies and your rabbit has simply decided to take your top rabbit spot over. A rabbit attempting to do this may urinate someplace your scent is especially strong—on your favorite chair or sofa or, worse, your bed or pillow. In this case you need to show you are keeping your spot as top rabbit. Clap your hands when he gets on the piece of furniture. If he does not get off of his own accord, lift him and put him onto the floor. You need to make it clear it is *your* piece of furniture. If it is your bed where he has decided to make his move, keeping the bedroom off-limits may work best.

A variation of the above problem can occur with other animals in the household. One of my rabbits always came down in the morning and jumped on the couch where I would sit with him and pet him while I drank my morning tea. Unfortunately, one of my cats decided it was fun to jump up on the couch and pester the rabbit. To show the cat the couch was *his* territory, the rabbit began urinating on the couch when the cat would jump up. I resolved this problem by spraying the cat with a water bottle every time she jumped on the couch with the rabbit. Given rabbits' stubbornness, I knew it would be much easier to change the cat's behavior than the rabbit's.

Mean or Aggressive Rabbit

When I first heard of mean rabbits I thought the phrase was rather funny. Who, after all, could imagine a mean *rabbit?* But I soon learned that an aggressive or mean rabbit is no joke. Rabbit bites can go clear through fingers, bone and all. Rabbit scratches are worse, in my opinion, than cat scratches. Some rabbits become so aggressive they will attack any person who enters a room, usually going for the ankles, and will chase, growl, chomp onto lower limbs and not let go. But such behavior is not a reason to get rid of your rabbit.

The first question to ask if you think you may have a mean rabbit is what are you calling aggressive behavior? If a rabbit nips you when you quit petting him or to get you to pay attention to him, this is not really aggressive behavior. It is one of the ways rabbits naturally communicate. Try teaching him not to bite too hard by squealing when his nips are too sharp. If the rabbit bites you or lunges at you when you reach into his cage, this too is acceptable rabbit behavior. The cage is his and he is letting you know that. But if you are talking about attacks, chases, and hard bites with no apparent provocation, you probably do have an aggressive rabbit.

The second question to ask if your rabbit exhibits aggressive behavior is if your rabbit is a young unaltered rabbit. Young rabbits, as they reach sexual maturity, may exhibit more aggressive behavior. This is true of both females and males, and the behavior usually leaves within a month or so after the rabbit is altered. My young Satin buck bit me every time I tried to pet him, although he would elicit the petting and was not otherwise an ill-tempered rabbit. This biting stopped within two weeks of having him neutered.

Another one of my rabbits, the sweetest, most loving little rabbit you could imagine, suddenly attacked my ankles one day. When he had chased me to the other side of the room, he stopped. But when I tried to cross the room he attacked again. Then I realized—my sweet little rabbit had recently reached sexual maturity and the other rabbit loose in the room was also a male. My rabbit, who had exhibited courtship behavior toward me, was driving me away from the other male in the room. Interestingly, he attacked me, not the other male.

When I removed the other buck from the room he stopped attacking me.

If your aggressive rabbit has already been spayed or neutered, you probably have a rabbit that was or is being disciplined in an inappropriate manner. Excessively aggressive behavior is usually an expression of excessive fear—the rabbit's fear that he will be hurt. If you raised the rabbit yourself ask yourself the following questions: Do you (or anyone else in your household) try to discipline your rabbit as you would a cat or a dog? Have you struck your rabbit with a newspaper or shouted at it? Do you have young rambunctious children whose behavior might seem threatening to your rabbit? Or a dog or cat whose play may be too rough and frighten your rabbit?

However a rabbit becomes aggressive, the best way to rehabilitate him is with acceptance. Do not compound the problem by trying to punish him for his behavior. Wear long pants, high-topped shoes or boots and gloves if necessary, and meet his aggressive actions with love. Admire him; tell him what a sweet wonderful rabbit he is. It will take time, possibly one or two months, but more than likely the rabbit will gradually respond to this method. As he or she slowly realizes there is nothing to fear from you or his environment, the rabbit will calm down and any charges toward you will be those of welcome.

Mounting

Anyone who is around rabbits for long comes to understand why for thousands of years hares and rabbits have been associated with homosexuality and transgenderism. In some parts of the world it was thought that rabbits changed sex every year. In other cultures it was believed that eating the flesh of a hare or rabbit would cause a person to become homosexual. No doubt these ideas arose because of the mounting behavior of lagomorphs. Mounting, by both sexes of both sexes, is common. It is a form of dominance. A rabbit exerting its dominance over another rabbit will often mount it, whether the other rabbit is the same sex or the opposite sex. I had one rabbit that was so convincing I feared I might have sexed it wrong and was going to end up with a litter of rabbit kittens! As with many other behaviors humans find unacceptable in rabbits, mounting will be greatly reduced by altering, although it may not cease entirely. This is another behavior a rabbit should never be shouted at or otherwise disciplined for. If the behavior offends or otherwise disturbs you, think about sticking to one rabbit.

Rabbits may also try mounting other animals, such as cats or humans. One woman I met said her cat didn't seem to mind it, so they just let it be. It can sometimes be embarrassing if your rabbit decides to mount you—especially in the presence of someone who is not a rabbit-savvy person. One of my buck rabbits tried to mount my arm every time I tried to pet him. Another preferred my leg. The behavior disappeared when they were neutered.

Fur Pulling

This behavior can be one of the most distressing to a rabbit owner, as the rabbit soon looks like a poor little waif and the excess hair consumed may also cause gastrointestinal problems. There are several things that can cause excessive fur pulling. One is an infestation of a parasite such as fur mites. Allergies may also cause a rabbit to pull his fur out. One rabbit owner found that the powder deodorizer she was using in her carpet made the rabbit itch and caused him to pull his fur out. An unspayed female may go through a false pregnancy and pull the fur from her chest for a nest.

But the most common cause of fur pulling, and one frequently unrecognized even by veterinarians, is maloccluded (misaligned) teeth. Rabbits with maloccluded teeth often pull fur excessively. It may be because they get hold of extra fur with the maloccluded teeth when grooming themselves. Or it may be because drooling which is often associated with maloccluded teeth leads to dermatitis on the chin and chest which itches and causes the rabbit to pull fur out. If your rabbit pulls fur excessively, check his teeth or have your vet check the teeth for any malocclusion.

A behavioral cause of excessive fur-pulling is boredom. Does your rabbit have enough toys in his cage? Do you spend enough time playing with him? If he is an only rabbit, perhaps he needs a rabbit companion.

Finally, fur-pulling behavior may start as a result of a stressful change to your rabbit. Have you stopped paying as much attention to him? Is there a new pet or person in the household? If one of these is the cause, reassuring the rabbit with extra attention may stop the fur-pulling behavior.

Whatever the cause of the fur-pulling, it will be necessary to watch the rabbit's diet as long as the behavior continues. Rabbits that pull their fur need extra fiber in their diet to keep the intestines healthy and moving. Give him plenty of hay and fresh vegetables and keep a close eye on his production of feces. If they become too small or stop altogether you may need to take your rabbit to the vet.

Withdrawal or Depression

Another problem which may arise with rabbits is withdrawal. A rabbit that becomes withdrawn may stop following its usual routine, hide, and fail to respond to your attention as he did before. As with other behavior changes, first eliminate any possible health condition as the reason. Check the rabbit's eyes and ears for discharge. Is the rabbit sniffing or snuffling or showing any other symptoms of disease?

If you find no signs of a health problem, the cause may be behavioral. Ask yourself the usual questions—have you moved things, brought new things into house? Is there a new person or pet in the house? Is it a busy time of year and are you paying your rabbit less attention without realizing it? Sometimes there may be subtle changes in our behavior toward a pet rabbit which we do not even detect but the rabbit does.

One of the most dramatic examples I know of regarding a change in owner behavior that adversely affected the rabbit was with my rabbit Muffy. I had gotten the young female Mini Lop as a companion for another rabbit. Muffy was very affectionate, although she would not tolerate being picked up. She did love to sit in my lap if she jumped there of her own accord, and she adored being petted. She was the sweetest little girl, very unlike the neutered male rabbit I had at the time. Then came the day to have her spayed, and it turned out "she" was "he!" I had taken the previous owner's word for it that the rabbit was a female, and because "she" hated being picked up, I had never attempted to verify the sex myself. Since "she" did not have the glaringly obvious genitals my other male had, nor displayed any of the spraying or other behavior I expected of a maturing male, I never even suspected "she" had been sexed wrong. Even the veterinarian hadn't noticed until time to operate!

The spay turned into a neuter. After the operation, Muffy stayed in the corner of his cage or hid under a table in the room, refused to play or behave in a normal fashion, and would not eat. At first I assumed it was a result of the stress of the operation, and after 24 hours had passed without him eating, I began to syringe-feed him. I was finally able to coax him to eat on his own, but he remained withdrawn. My sweet, outgoing Muffy-rabbit had changed drastically. When a full week had passed and there was no sign of this new behavior abating, I began to get worried. Then it finally dawned on me—had I somehow changed my treatment of him when I realized he was a he and not a she? It was true that instead of saying "There's my sweet Muffy-girl, O sweet Muffy girl" I was now saying "There's my cute little Muffin boy. Little Muffin boy." I couldn't see much difference, but did he? Were there other changes in my behavior toward him that I could not detect but Muffy could? I determined to treat Muffy as though I didn't know "she" was a "he." The next time I walked into the room, I went over to his cage and spoke in my old formula: "There's my sweet Muffy-girl. O sweet little Muffy girl." Muffy's reaction was amazing. "She" bounded over to the bars of "her" cage and pressed her nose through, anxious to be petted, back to her normal self. "She" has been fine since.

rabbits and other pets

Rabbit–Rabbit Bonding

Most rabbit aficionados end up with more than one. They are such delightful, fun, and loving pets; how can you possibly resist adopting another? And if you have to work, you don't like to think of your rabbit alone in a cage all day. But not all rabbits love each other at once. It may take time for them to bond, if they do. It is often recommended that a person stick to neutered-male spayed female pairings. While these may have a higher rate of success, the truth is that any mix of sex (and size) can work. In fact, my most bonded rabbits are a female-female pair in which I broke all the rules. I took a pair of unrelated, unspayed females (a Dutch and a Holland Lop) and threw them together with no preparation. They became so strongly bonded that I never had to separate them; not even during the time when they had reached sexual maturity but were too

Bringing in a second rabbit may cause some stress for the first. These two rabbits don't always get along as well as this picture implies.

young to spay. This was sheer luck, though, and the chances of rabbits getting along can be maximized by introducing them carefully.

When you first bring the new rabbit home, don't put it in your current rabbit's space. Put it somewhere that is not part of your first rabbit's territory. Let them smell each other through the door for a few days. This helps the new rabbit, too. Then after two or three days, have them meet in a neutral place. Sometimes the bathroom or a bedroom where no other bunnies live works well for this purpose. You should have a heavy book and a pair of thick gloves ready. Put the rabbits at opposite ends of an open space in the room and then stay with them and watch. The rabbits will usually stretch forward, neck out, ears up and at a slight V, and sniff. (With lop rabbits the ears will swing forward.) If your rabbits then proceed to ignore each other, good. They are accepting each other's presence. If they circle, chase, and mount one another, they are establishing their dominance, and this is OK too. If they groom each other, you're there! Return the rabbits to their separate areas and repeat the process each day until you are certain the rabbits are going to get along.

However, instead of the above you may end up with a serious fight, and if this happens you must be prepared to separate the rabbits! A serious rabbit fight can end in severe injury or even death. Fighting rabbits will bite and kick, ripping at the other's face, underbelly, and genital area. Truly fighting rabbits move so rapidly they look like one big rotating ball of fur. First try to stop them by clapping or dropping the book to startle them. If that doesn't work you will have to physically separate them. (Some people recommend using brooms or other items to separate fighting rabbits, but in my opinion that can risk injury to the rabbits.) Put your gloves on, reach down, and try to get hold of one of them. You must have gloves—one of my fingers was bitten completely through when I was trying to separate a pair of fighting rabbits. After you have managed to catch one of the rabbits, return them to their separate rooms and try introducing them again the next day.

For a very fortunate few, the process of bonding rabbits is instant, because it is love at first sight. More likely though, it will take from two weeks to two months. If you have difficulty getting two rabbits to bond, there are a few tricks some people have had success with. One of the most often recommended is to force the rabbits to share a new and frightening (to them) experience together, such as a ride in a car. Put them in a box together, or a two-compartment transport cage

These three Mini Lops are quite comfortable together.

with a wire divider, and take them for a ride. By the time they get back, they may be friends, or at least accept each other's presence. Another rabbit owner suggests having the rabbits on harness and leash so they can be restrained and prevented from getting in a serious fight.

Remember that some fighting among rabbits is natural. Because of their natures they will engage in scuffles to remind each other of their places in the scheme of things, and you will probably find bits of fur that have been pulled out. However, if your rabbits are engaging in more serious fights with aggressive chasing and bites that are causing injury, you should not leave them in a cage together unattended. In a small space where the rabbits cannot get away serious injury or death could occur from a fight.

There are some rabbits that will never bond. Rabbits, like people, may take violent likes or dislikes to others of their kind. If a rabbit appears to be unable to tolerate another, the best thing to do is accept the situation and adapt. One of my nine rabbits will not bond to any of my others. So his time out of his cage is when the rest of the rabbits are confined. My solitary rabbit enjoys going around and sniffing at the other rabbits in their cages, and appears to think he is the top rabbit who keeps all the others in their place. Maybe he is!

Introducing Rabbits and Pets of Other Species

If you already have pets of other species when you adopt your rabbit, introducing them should wait until the rabbit feels secure. Let him explore the room you are keeping him in and become comfortable with his environment before introducing your other pets. The rabbit will, of course, have some knowledge of the other pets' presence in the house because he will smell them and probably hear them. But if he does not yet see them he will be more comfortable and settle in sooner.

The following suggestions are for in-troducing rabbits to cats or dogs. The same recommendations can be followed with ferrets, although if you own a ferret you should be aware that some rabbits are never able to be in the presence of a ferret without becoming fearful. If your other pet is a guinea pig or hamster, the process of introductions can be speeded up, and it is the rabbit that should be watched for signs of aggression toward the smaller animal.

I would recommend waiting until your rabbit has been in his new home three days to a week before the initial meeting with a pet cat or dog. During this time the rabbit should be kept in a room where the cat or dog is not allowed. When your rabbit appears quite comfortable in his new home, it is time for him to meet the family cat or dog. Some people recommend having the first meeting in a neutral place that is not the territory of either pet. Although I agree with this method for rabbits meeting rabbits, I do not think it necessary for rabbits meeting cats or dogs. By the time several days to a week has passed they are aware of each other's presence already through smell and sound. I recommend leaving the rabbit in his cage in its usual spot and then allowing the cat or dog (not the two at once if you have both) into the same room for a few minutes. Stay in the room the entire time and watch things closely. The cat or dog will likely go up to the cage and sniff at the rabbit, which will probably sniff back. Watch the rabbit closely. If he appears excessively frightened—if he flattens himself, eyes bulging, or begins to thump—remove the other pet from the room immediately. If your other pet is a dog, try to keep it from barking, as this can often frighten a rabbit. After about fifteen minutes, remove the other pet from the room. Repeat the process each day, lengthening the time about fifteen minutes a day, for five days to a week or until the animals appear comfortable with each other's presence. Be sure you pay attention to both animals during these initial visits, letting both see that the other is a member of the family.

It is now time to have the rabbit meet the other pet out of his cage. Let the rabbit loose in the room first, leaving his cage door open so he can retreat if he feels he needs to. Then bring the cat or dog into the room (preferably on a leash). While keeping the cat or dog under firm control, allow the rabbit to come forward and meet the other pet. He will most likely approach slowly, ears pointing forward, hindquarters up, tail pointing back. Should the rabbit's posture change to ears back and tail up like a flag, remove the cat or dog immediately, as the rabbit may be getting ready to lunge forward and bite. Fifteen minutes is long enough for the first visit. Repeat this for a day or two more, and if all is going well, you can allow the cat or dog in the room with the rabbit without being under restraint.

Unexpected problems can arise when a household contains rabbits and cats or dogs. My brother's golden retriever persisted in hanging around close to my rabbits' cage. The dog did not behave in a threatening manner, but his very presence upset my rabbits. It took me a day or two to realize the dog insisted on staying by the cage because he was watching for delicious treats to fall from the cage—bunny feces. (I found this hilarious, but my brother did not.) One of my cats also hung around rabbit cages, but with less benign intentions. She enjoyed sticking her paw through the bars and teasing the rabbits. Squirts from a water bottle taught the cat this was not acceptable behavior.

Sometimes, friendships may develop between cats

or dogs and rabbits. They may sleep together and even play together. One game rabbits and dogs or cats may play is "chase." Often the rabbit appears to enjoy this, and may turn and chase the cat or dog in return. However, these "games" should always be watched closely, as they

**Barkley and Sebastian.
A dog and a rabbit can be friends, but should never be left together unsupervised.**

can suddenly turn into tragedy. Some dogs, in particular, may chase too often or aggressively and need to be taught to leave the rabbit alone. Anne McBride's book, *Why does my rabbit...?*, in-cludes an excellent section on teaching a dog the command "leave," which is then used to order the dog away from the rabbit.

Please remember, however: *No matter how well a rabbit and cat or dog get along, never leave them both free and unattended.* It only takes a moment, and your rabbit may be seriously injured or dead.

Bully Bunnies

Anyone who has had rabbits knows they are not all sweetness and light. One of the rather unexpected situations that can develop when you have rabbits and pets of other species is when the rabbit bullies the other animal. This most often happens when the other pet is a guinea pig, but, surprisingly, it can also happen with cats, and occasionally even with dogs. Rabbits have been known to chase, kick, and bite cats and dogs. When you do end up with a bunny bully, it can be a difficult situation to resolve. Rabbits are very concerned with establishing a social order in their environment, and if the rabbit has decided he is going to be the top pet, it is hard to stop. You can try spraying the rabbit with a water bottle when he attacks the other animal, or clapping your hands, or giving a short screech. But if none of your efforts work, you may just have to keep them separated.

But It Can All Work

If the above sections leave you feeling pessimistic about rabbits getting along with other animals, let me assure you it can all work. Rabbits and guinea pigs frequently get along just fine. Rabbits and cats sometimes become so bonded they sleep together in the rabbit's cage and follow each other around the house. Dogs may even guard household rabbits, placing themselves in a protective stance between the

Cats and rabbit sit companionably and watch the outside world.

rabbits and new people or strange dogs.

I would like to share the following story sent to me by another rabbit person:

"My parents inherited a pet bunny when my brother returned home from college. (They already had an old cat and a young dog—both of whom were house pets.) This bunny was a house bunny and gradually all the animals learned to live together, and the bunny even learned that he was allowed only in the kitchen and TV rooms (living room and dining room were off-limits to him). He spent most of his day in his cage in the kitchen, but was allowed playtime every evening when the family was home to supervise.

"The most remarkable aspect of the bunny's place in their home developed when my father had his second open-heart surgery. Upon returning home for his recovery, my dad was at home all day, and in time, he would be left alone, as my mom and brother were running the family business. My mom thought she had seen everything when she returned home from work one afternoon to find my dad asleep on the chaise lounge on the porch, the dog between his legs, cat on one arm, and the rabbit on the pillow next to his head! It was not a one-time deal, either. My dad reported that this was the normal routine for his afternoon nap!

"And they say dogs, cats, and rabbits are mortal enemies! Ha! These three musketeers got along and all shared the companionship and nursing duties of my dad while he was recovering, and then continued to live together for several years."

caring for older and special needs rabbits

caring for older and special needs rabbits takes time, patience, money, and skill, but the rewards are commensurate with the investment. Some of the most loving and affectionate rabbits are those that are elderly or have health problems. Even if you start out with a young healthy rabbit, it may develop health problems at some point in its life, and if your rabbit has the long life you hope it will, it will eventually develop some of the signs of age. Or, if you have the time, patience, and some previous experience with rabbits, you may choose to adopt a rabbit that is already older or has special needs.

older rabbits

As with other mammals, the changes of age come gradually. Your rabbit will slow down—not run as much, or jump as high. It may have trouble getting into its litter box and need one with one lower sides. He or she will probably sleep more, and seek out soft spots more than before. He will probably like it a little warmer and he may not be able to hop up the stairs. Some of his fur will turn white, and it will thin. He may well have several

Older rabbits often slow down and like to snuggle.

years left though, and you should enjoy this slower time with your rabbit. You may now have the television companion who likes to cuddle on your lap that you only dreamed of when he was younger and more active.

There are a few health problems that may develop during these years and which you should watch for. Most of them are minor and can be dealt with relatively easily, but a few could become serious problems.

Teeth

Your older rabbit will not eat as much or chew things as much, and this can lead to overgrowth of the teeth. Check the teeth weekly, and look for sores and swelling in the mouth. Encourage him to eat. Sometimes it helps to provide bite-sized treats such as a chopped up apple or carrot. Try coaxing him to chew on fresh unsprayed willow or apple twigs. If the teeth do overgrow, you will need to have them trimmed or burred.

Ears

Older rabbits often develop warts on their ears. Although these look rather awful, they do not usually cause a health problem, and are generally left untreated. Rabbits may also experience some hearing loss from unrecognized ear infection. Hearing loss often goes unnoticed in older rabbits, and usually causes no problems other than an unusual aggressiveness if the rabbit is startled by someone approaching him unseen.

Eyes

Older rabbits may develop cataracts or glaucoma. Cataracts can sometimes be treated with laser surgery. Usually, however, the rabbit adapts to his gradually lessening vision and the cataracts are not treated. Glaucoma is often not recognized in a rabbit until irreversible damage has already occurred to the optic nerve. Glaucoma is not painful to rabbits, and it will usually not be treated. Rabbits who lose their vision to either condition will usually adapt quite well. They may still run around the house and keep most of their former habits. It will help a visually impaired rabbit if the house is kept neat and things are not moved so he does not run into something he does not expect to be there.

Note—white New Zealand rabbits sometimes develop an inherited glaucoma very early in life. Like older rabbits, they are usually able to adapt quite well to vision loss.

Nails

The nails on a rabbit's paws may start to turn outward with age. Keeping them trimmed usually prevents any problems from developing, but you will need to watch for any nails that get torn from the paw and might become infected.

Elimination Problems

Older rabbits may have difficulty hopping into high-sided litter boxes. Cut one side down or purchase low-sided cat litter boxes. Older rabbits may also need to have more litter boxes available so they can make it to the box in time. Sometimes arthritis may prevent a rabbit from bending back to clean its anal area properly. If this occurs, you will have to help the rabbit keep the area clean. If the fur becomes matted with droppings, carefully clip the hair away and then clean the area with a soft damp cloth. Keeping the fur around the anal area trimmed down will help. If the rabbit is also unable to reach and consume his cecotrophs, you will need to collect them and feed them to him.

Ileus

As your rabbit grows older, eats less, and is less active, he is at high risk for developing ileus, or a slowdown of the intestinal tract (also called gastrointestinal or GI stasis). This can be a very dangerous condition for rabbits. Learn to recognize the major signs of ileus: painful gas, small droppings or no droppings, loss of appetite. Treat the rabbit with simethicone for the gas (see Chapter 10), try to coax him to eat grass hay, and give him plenty of fluids. See Chapter 12 for more information on ileus.

Urolithiasis

Sludge and stones in the urinary tract (see Chapter 12) are more common in older rabbits. Be sure your elder rabbit always has plenty of fresh water to drink. Try to reduce the amount of calcium in your rabbit's diet if you notice sludge in your rabbit's urine, as this may contribute toward the condition. Alfalfa is high in calcium and should be eliminated from the diet if possible. Stones may sometimes require manual expression of the bladder. See instructions for doing this under the section on special needs rabbits in this chapter.

Arthritis

Most older rabbits will develop arthritis to some degree, and sometimes total fusion of a joint affected by arthritis may occur. Your arthritis-affected rabbit won't be able to move around as easily, and may experience some pain. Try to make the rabbit's environment more comfortable. He may want it a little warmer, and need ramps to reach his favorite napping place or soft rugs to rest on. He may need help grooming himself and also need to be fed his cecotrophs if he cannot bend to reach them. If pain from arthritis is apparent in your rabbit, ask your vet about giving your rabbit half an 81 mg children's aspirin twice a day (for a five- to six-pound rabbit). Many rabbits will eat the cherry-flavored children's aspirin as though it is a treat.

Osteoporosis

Just like older humans, rabbits can develop osteoporosis if they receive inadequate calcium in their diets and don't exercise enough. While this can occur at any age, you should take extra care to protect your older rabbit. Osteoporosis can be a particularly dangerous condition for rabbits because it can lead to fracture of the spine. If your older rabbit's urine does not have sludge (see entry for urolithiasis above), give him a few high-calcium treats such as carrot tops or rolled oats.

Spondylosis of the Spine

This is a condition where bony protrusions develop on

the vertebrae. These spurs may bridge over to other vertebrae and fuse. During the years these develop your rabbit may sometimes experience pain when the spurs rub
against each other. A rabbit with this condition will slow
down and may eventually shuffle instead of hop or be
reluctant to move at all. He may have difficulty grooming
himself, especially around the anal area, and you will
have to do it for him. If he cannot reach his cecotrophs,
you will need to hand-feed them. You will also need to
make the rabbit's environment more comfortable and
accessible, and address the pain. Talk to your veterinarian
about aspirin or other analgesics. This condition is more
common in large rabbit breeds and overweight rabbits.

Cancer

With the exception of uterine cancer in unspayed
female rabbits, cancer is not a particularly common disease in rabbits, although it does occur. Spaying a female
rabbit before two years of age is the best way to prevent
uterine cancer. The risks of mammary and testicular cancer are reduced by spaying or neutering your rabbit.
Lymphoma usually occurs in younger rabbits. Squamous
cell cancer may develop from horny warts in older rabbits, and other cancers may occur rarely. Watch for any
unusual growths and have them checked.

Arteriosclerosis

This is a thickening or hardening of artery walls. Rabbits
fed diets high in fats may be at risk for this happening
from fatty deposits (atherosclerosis). Diets high in calcium may contribute toward mineralization of the arter-
ies. Signs of arteriosclerosis include lethargy, anorexia,

convulsions, and/or sudden death. The best way to prevent this is to feed your rabbit a healthy diet low in fat and not too high in calcium (remember your rabbit needs *adequate* calcium to prevent osteoporosis).

Strokes

Strokes are caused by the obstruction of the blood flow through a vessel in the brain, or the rupture of a vessel in the brain. They are rare in rabbits. There is no treatment. Intensive nursing with fluids and analgesics may help. The rabbit may become incontinent and need manual expression of the bladder.

tips on caring for special needs rabbits

Caring for special needs rabbits can be a sensitive issue. Some people feel that keeping disabled rabbits alive is cruel and inhumane. Those who devote themselves to a special needs rabbit and are rewarded by seeing it exhibit the behavior of a happy or content rabbit feel beyond doubt that they have made the correct choice. I know I would

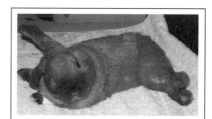

This special needs rabbit with deformed hind legs is wonderfully good natured and impossible not to love.

not trade the times my special needs rabbit hums around the room, licks my face, and even tries to kick his heels for anything.

Special needs rabbits include those suffering from a variety of diseases and conditions. Splayleg, stroke, broken back, maloccluded teeth, chronic bacterial infection, recurring abscesses, cancer, and encephalitozoonosis are just a few of the conditions that may require a rabbit to have long-term special care. The specific needs of the rabbit will vary depending on the nature of the condition.

Attitude

Be prepared for changes in your special needs rabbit's personality. Like people who are ill, rabbits who are ill will also have good and bad days and their attitudes will reflect this. A rabbit that has never bitten may suddenly take a chunk out of your finger while you are attempting to clean him or otherwise attend to his needs. A rabbit that usually has a happy, outgoing personality may stay quietly in a corner of his cage for a day or two. A normally sweet-tempered rabbit may throw a tantrum and fling dishes around or bang toys on the floor. Remember how you behaved last time you had a bad cold or serious toothache and accept these behavioral reflections of your rabbit's level of well-being as you would a person's.

Companion Rabbit

Many rabbit owners have reported a dramatic change in their special needs rabbit's attitude when they got a caretaker rabbit. A caretaker rabbit is essentially a rabbit with an earth mother type personality, and may be either a male or female. (Of course, this is only feasible if your special needs rabbit does not have a condition that is contagious.) Some shelters may have rabbits they know of with this personality, as may some rabbit-fostering groups. Call your local rabbit rescue group or shelter and ask. If you explain what you are looking for, they may be able to recommend a particular rabbit and they will often allow you to take the prospective caretaker rabbit on a trial basis before committing to another adoption.

Cage Size

Sometimes with special needs rabbits upsizing or downsizing the cage may help. If the rabbit needs to be able to stretch way out and cannot be out of his cage as often as in the past, a bigger cage may help. In other cases downsizing a cage may help. My special needs rabbit started out in a 3'×2' cage. Cleaning this large cage for my tiny, frequently incontinent rabbit took me a minimum of 45 minutes a day (not to mention the time spent cleaning the rabbit). For this admittedly selfish reason, I downsized his cage with unexpected results. My timid sweet little special needs rabbit *liked* his much smaller cage. He clearly felt more secure in it, and the time I had to spend cleaning it was now reduced to 10 minutes. This extra time of mine went to extra attention and longer time out of his cage for Timothy, who really began to thrive.

Mobile Platforms

Some owners of elder rabbits and special needs rabbits have built special mobile platforms for their rabbits to be on during the day. These platforms should be about 2'×3' for smaller rabbits and 3'×4' for larger ones. A rim about two to three inches high is affixed to the platform, and wheels fastened to the bottom. With the addition of a low-sided litter box, soft bedding, and food dishes, the disabled rabbit now has his own "room" which can be wheeled from place to place so he can be included in the activities of his home.

Bedding

Special needs rabbits will often require extra-soft bedding. Sheepskins work well, as do thick quilts. Rabbits with paralyzed limbs will need egg crate foam underneath their bedding to prevent the formation of pressure sores.

Rabbit Carts

Rabbits with paralyzed hindquarters due to broken backs and certain illnesses can be given an enhanced quality of life by fitting them with a cart. The cart will support the rabbit's hindquarters, and it is able to pull itself forward with its front legs. Not all rabbits will adapt to this, but many do. Talk to your veterinarian about this option. The K9 Cart Company (address listed in Appendix I) makes rabbit-sized carts.

Rabbit Diapers

Many special needs rabbits are incontinent. This creates problems for both the owner and the rabbit. Incontinent rabbits will often develop hutch burn (see Chapter 12). Fitting the rabbit with diapers may help both rabbit and owner. Rabbits may object to the diapers at first, but the increased comfort leads many to accept them with time. The winter 2000 issue of *The Bunny Thymes* has an article explaining how to diaper a rabbit. Purchase a small disposable baby diaper. Cut a tail hole just above the middle of the diaper. Cut two slits above the diaper tabs, angling them away from the tabs into the diaper. Attach the tabs over the back of the rabbit, fit the tail in the hole, and tape the diaper in place or secure it with an elastic bandage with Velcro fastenings.

Manual Expression of the Bladder

Several conditions of rabbits may require that you learn to manually push the urine from the rabbit's bladder, although you should never do this unless specifically instructed to do so by your veterinarian. Rupture of the bladder can occur if a urolith (stone) is lodged where it effectively blocks any urine from draining from the bladder.

Procedure: First hold the rabbit over the sink, tail away from you. Try pouring some warm water over the urethra. This will sometimes cause the rabbit to urinate. If he does not, place your hand on his stomach just below the rib cage and then press gently backwards toward his tail. The urine should squirt out.

Cleaning Rabbits

Although it is never a good idea to bathe your rabbit unless it is absolutely necessary, you will sometimes have to clean a special needs rabbit. Urine-soaked fur can be cleaned with warm water or Chlorhexiderm Flush®, which has a drying agent. Feces can also be cleaned off with warm water. If it is caked on, Novalsan® Otic Solution (for cleaning ears) can be used to soften the feces for removal. Always hold the rabbit gently but firmly and take your time cleaning the rabbit so it does not become stressed or hurt itself trying to get away. It will take time—one woman I spoke to told me it takes her 45 minutes every morning to clean her special needs rabbit whose hindquarters are paralyzed. Always dry your rabbit well after any washing. Clipping the fur around the anal area will also help keep the rabbit clean.

Trimming Teeth

One of the most common conditions in both elder and special needs rabbits is overgrown or maloccluded incisors which need to be trimmed. Veterinarians differ as to the best method for trimming teeth. Some prefer clipping and others prefer burring. The truth is that each method has its advantages and disadvantages. However, most rabbit owners do not have the knowledge or equipment for burring a rabbit's teeth, while they can learn to clip a rabbit's teeth. Good quality toenail clippers can be used to trim the teeth of smaller rabbits, as can guillotine-style cat nail cutters. For larger rabbits, you may wish to purchase teeth-trimming tools specifically made for rabbits.

Hold the rabbit firmly upside down or wrap him in a towel (it helps if you have someone to assist you), pull the lips away, and cut firmly and rapidly, releasing the cutters quickly. Do not hold onto the teeth with the cutters or pull, as the teeth can be accidentally jerked out or fractured. Serious infections can develop if a tooth fractures below the gum line. Also be careful not to cut the gums, tongue, or cheeks. Pieces of tooth should be removed from the rabbit's mouth so he does not swallow them. A cotton swab can be used to remove smaller pieces. If you have an older rabbit whose teeth are merely overgrown, you need only trim off a little. If you have a rabbit with severely maloccluded teeth, you can trim the lower incisors to just above the gum line (they will grow back very rapidly). Trim the upper incisors just far enough so they do not curve back dangerously (upper incisors can curve back so far they pierce the palate). If you are uncomfortable trimming the rabbit's teeth yourself or find it too difficult, have a veterinarian trim them or show you how to trim them.

emotional considerations

If you choose to care for an older or special needs rabbit, there will be emotional costs as well as time and financial costs. There will be days your rabbit seems almost like his or her old self, and others when whatever you do does not seem to relieve your pet's discomfort. The pain of these latter times will most likely be offset by the close bond

Brambley Hedge Rabbit Rescue. Call your local rabbit rescue if you have a rabbit you don't know how to take care of or need a caretaker rabbit.

you will develop with your rabbit. Many people have reported developing incredibly close relationships with their ailing rabbits—much closer than during the animals' young and healthy years. Treasure this closeness and allow it to give you the strength and patience for the trying and painful times.

A person who chooses to adopt a special needs or

older rabbit has had time to consider the costs and is ready to take them on. But when a person's healthy rabbit becomes ill or disabled, the owner has a difficult decision to make. Take time to make the decision. Consult with a trusted veterinarian, consider the quality of life the rabbit will have, and weigh the emotional, time, and financial costs to yourself. Caring for disabled or ill rabbits is not easy. For example, a rabbit with a broken back may require a special cart to get around, have to be cleaned frequently, and be constantly checked for the development of pressure sores. Despite one's compassion, there will be times that even the most patient person will become tired of cleaning up messes and/or saying no to yet another invitation out because the rabbit cannot be left alone for long.

Don't forget to consider the individual rabbit when making your decision. Is the rabbit a fighter who appears to want to live? Does he still exhibit behavior that is consistent with a happy or content rabbit? Above all, be honest with yourself when trying to make the difficult decision of whether or not to take on the care of a seriously ill or disabled rabbit. If you feel you are unable to take the burden on because of your job or the emotional or financial costs, admit it. There is nothing wrong with that. Not everyone is able to care for special needs rabbits. If you feel you cannot, contact a local rabbit rescue organization or chapter of the House Rabbit Society and discuss options with them.

Be prepared for disapproval from some people if you do choose to care for an older or special needs rabbit. This may come whether you are caring for a severely disabled rabbit or one with a relatively minor problem. I once overheard a rabbit breeder telling another woman that any rabbit with maloccluded teeth should be put down. A rabbit with maloccluded teeth would be miserable and in pain all the time and come to hate life and its owner, the woman claimed. She added that to have the condition treated by a veterinarian would cost thousands. I could tell she was absolutely convinced she was correct, and when she learned I had a rabbit with splayleg and severely maloccluded teeth, her disapproval was plain.

I chose not to argue with the woman, but I knew she was wrong. I know the behavior of a happy and contented rabbit, and that is the behavior my rabbit with maloccluded teeth displays most of the time. He is unable to jump as other rabbits do, but under my care the strength of his hind legs has improved greatly. When I enter a room where he is, he runs over to me and stands on his splayed hind legs, begging to be petted. Morning and evening he runs about humming and even kicking his hind feet. This is not a rabbit that hates me and hates life! Yes, he does experience a short period of discomfort when his teeth are trimmed, and he sometimes develops dermatitis on his chin, which causes him some discomfort, but these times are few. And as for costing thousands to treat it, it usually costs less than $30 per month to have a veterinarian trim the teeth. As Kathy Smith, the author of *Rabbit Health in the 21st Century: A Guide for Bunny Parents,* so aptly pointed out, the cost is offset by the savings in property damage since rabbits with maloccluded teeth don't destroy things by chewing.

If you are caring for a severely disabled or

terminally ill rabbit, the disapproval may be stronger and come even from those closest to you. Once when one of my pets was dying I choose not to euthanize her but to allow her to "die naturally." I made this decision based on my knowledge of my pet and the

Baby Girl, a rabbit with head tilt, runs and jumps and insists on acting like a normal rabbit.

assurances of my vet that she was not in pain, but was "slowly fading away." It took about six weeks, and the time was made more difficult for me because of the clear disapproval of friends and even family. One friend bluntly told me he thought it would be more humane to euthanize her.

My question was, more humane for whom? Not for my pet, who was still displaying behaviors consistent with some enjoyment of life, or for me, who needed the last days to come to terms with my loss. I realized that the answer to my question was more humane for the friends and family who were uncomfortable facing the reality of death. I did what I felt was right, and have been thankful for it. The caretakers of elder and special needs rabbits should listen to themselves, not others. Do what you know is right for you and your rabbit.

Saying Goodbye

Most of us who take a pet rabbit into our homes will have to face that pet's death sooner or later. Loss is the price of love. We may expect it, as with an older or seriously ill rabbit, or it may come unexpectedly to a rabbit that was perfectly healthy the day before.

Sometimes, if the rabbit is in great pain and there is little or no hope of recovery, we may choose to hasten death through euthanasia. Always make this decision in conjunction with your veterinarian, but do not allow it to be made for you. If euthanasia does appear to be the kindest choice for your rabbit, you will need to decide whether or not to be present during the procedure, should your vet allow it. If you do choose to be present, there are things you should be aware of. One is that there may be visible muscle spasms. Another is that death occurs quite rapidly after the euthanasia agent is administered. Sally Walshaw, in the *BSAVA Manual of Rabbit Medicine and Surgery,* recommends giving the rabbit a subcutaneous anesthetic (such as a combination of ketamine and xylazine) first. This can help calm a suffering or frightened animal, and also reduces the likelihood of the involuntary muscle spasms.

However death comes to your rabbit, the days following will probably be a very difficult time. Guilt is often a particularly strong aspect of grief after the death of a pet rabbit because many rabbit owners do fail to recognize illnesses and other medical conditions or to respond to them in the appropriate manner. I have done that myself. If you feel your rabbit died because of a mistake you made, you should first admit it to yourself. Then forgive yourself. Realize it is understandable—rabbits are still uncommon pets, and owners simply don't know as much about them as they do cats and dogs. Take comfort from the fact that you won't make the same mistake with your next rabbit. Share your experience online to help other new rabbit owners avoid making the same errors.

Be prepared for friends and family not to fully comprehend your grief upon the death of your rabbit. It is a curious fact that even people who understand grieving for a pet cat or dog do not understand the depth of grief a person may experience upon losing a beloved rabbit. Small companion animals are seen somehow as "disposable pets," and it is surprising to some people that anyone would grieve much for them at all, let alone grieve deeply for a long period of time. If this is the attitude of family and friends, first be honest. Tell them how you feel. If they are still unable to empathize with you, limit your contact with them or avoid discussing your rabbit's death with them for awhile. It will only make you more upset.

The most important thing to do is to allow yourself to grieve and to realize it will take time to go through the grieving process. It can take up to a full year to recover from a significant loss, and if a person is deeply attached to their pet rabbit, the loss is a significant one. The time to recover will also be influenced by other things in a person's life—job, family, friends, any other losses experienced during the same time period. Some people find comfort in communicating with people on the Internet who do understand. Many rabbit Web sites and animal sanctuary sites have pages where a person can exchange messages with someone who has experienced a similar loss or where a tribute to a pet that has passed on or "gone over the rainbow bridge" can be posted.

Depending upon your religious background, you may also find comfort in burying your rabbit in your yard or at a pet memorial park. Others prefer to have their pets cremated and scatter the ashes in a meaningful place. Still others have a simple shrine in their house with a picture of the rabbit, a candle and/or flowers, and perhaps a favorite toy. Planting a tree, rosebush, or other flowering shrub in memory of the rabbit or giving a donation to a rabbit welfare organization helps some grieving pet owners come to terms with their loss. Do whatever helps you the most. Then, in time, you will have the courage to open your heart to another rabbit.

If you have another rabbit that was bonded to the one who died, don't forget that rabbit will also be experiencing loss and will need extra care. Some rabbit caregivers strongly recommend that the surviving partner be allowed to spend a little time with the body. Rabbits allowed to do this appear to comprehend the loss better and spend less time searching for their absent friends. You can also help by spending extra time with the surviving rabbit. Make a point of stopping and petting him every time you pass his cage. If his appetite declines, tempt him with special treats. After some time has passed, the surviving rabbit, like you, will probably be happiest if a new rabbit friend is brought into his life.

part two

rabbit health and medicine

The information in this section is not meant to substitute for competent veterinary care. It is provided so that rabbit owners may educate themselves to recognize signs of illness in their pets, and in emergency situations, know what to do to give their pets the best chance to survive.

rabbits, veterinarians, medications, and surgery

for many years, rabbits were considered by both owners and veterinarians alike to be very fragile animals that did not respond well to medications or surgical intervention. Fortunately, as the number of pet rabbits has increased, so have advances in treating them. Just a few years ago the average life span of a medium-sized pet rabbit was five to six years. Now it is eight to 10 years. Some live even longer.

However, not all veterinarians have kept up with the advances in rabbit medicine and surgery. It is important for the rabbit owner to be aware of the difficulties faced in treating rabbits and what is and is not safe for their pets.

finding a rabbit-savvy veterinarian

Finding a good, rabbit-savvy veterinarian can be difficult, and it is an unfortunate reality that at times the rabbit owner will find himself or herself in the uncomfortable position of knowing more about some aspects of rabbit care than his or her veterinarian. Most veterinary schools devote more instruction time to rabbit medicine now than in the past, and there are continuing education workshops and seminars on rabbit health and behavior available for practicing veterinarians, but many vets simply don't have much experience with rabbits. Others have had experience, but it may have been more oriented toward rabbits being raised commercially than those kept as much-loved pets. *Finding a good rabbit veterinarian is key to the long life and health of your pet rabbit.* Take time to call the offices of listed veterinarians and ask questions about the number of rabbits treated at the practice. Rabbits are considered "exotics," so you may have more luck with veterinarians who state they treat exotics in their ads. Recent graduates from veterinary school may be more knowledgeable about rabbits since many schools provide more instruction on rabbit medicine now than before. Ask friends who own rabbits what veterinarian they use and how well they like him or her. If you already have a vet for another pet, remember that an excellent dog and cat veterinarian will not necessarily be a good rabbit vet. Again, ask questions about his or her experience with rabbits. Don't let the DVM following the name intimidate you.

When you do find a veterinarian you think will be good with your rabbit, you will still not be able to relax. It has happened that veterinarians who did not have experience with rabbits have claimed to; either because they felt treating a rabbit wouldn't be that much different than treating a cat or dog, or because they simply wanted the money. If you are unfortunate enough to get one of these, you will need to be able to tell. There are a few danger signs to watch for when your rabbit is treated. A veterinarian should never prescribe lincomycin, clindamycin, or amoxicillin (also spelled amoxycillin) for a rabbit. This last medication is commonly used in treating cats. Although rarely a rabbit may tolerate the drug, others have died from a single dose. Other synthetic penicillins and oral penicillins such as ampicillin should not be prescribed either. They depress the appetite dangerously and a fatal diarrhea often develops after they are given to rabbits. There are diseases in rabbits which will require treatment with penicillin, but the drug should not be given orally and measures should be taken to protect the rabbit's delicate digestive system.

Also beware if your veterinarian tells you to withhold food and water from your rabbit for several hours before surgery. This is commonly done with cats and dogs to reduce the danger of vomiting. Vomiting is not a problem for rabbits, however, and it is more dangerous for their digestive tracts to be empty before surgery, particularly since it may take time to coax rabbits to eat after the surgery. For rabbits, it is only necessary to remove food and water an hour or so before the surgery so no food is in the mouth or esophagus and will not be aspirated into the trachea. Some vets may also worry about spaying a female rabbit when the cecum is full. However, it would take days with no food for the rabbit's cecum to empty, and the rabbit would die from the complications of going without food that long.

Once you have found a good, rabbit-savvy veterinarian, you have to start the whole process over and find another! There are several reasons you might not be able to reach your regular veterinarian when you need to. He or she might be on vacation, attending a conference, or simply not have emergency service late nights, weekends, or holidays. Please do not fail to locate an emergency vet ahead of time. I failed to do this myself once, and came to regret it. A much-beloved rabbit of mine became ill on a Saturday. I had known my regular vet did not have weekend or holiday service, but had not located an alternate. By Sunday morning I could tell my rabbit was seriously ill, and was frantically calling down the list of veterinarians in the telephone book, trying to find one who would see my rabbit. Only one agreed to see him, and she admitted straight up she did not have much experience with rabbits. I described the symptoms to her, and she told me that these were not critical symptoms in cats and dogs and that she thought my rabbit would be fine until she could see him later that morning. I knew my rabbit was critically ill, and continued my frantic calling, hoping to find a vet who would see my rabbit sooner. He died 10 minutes later.

As it turned out, my rabbit had acute bloat and volvulus and probably would have died even with surgical intervention. But it is hard to know that my failure to locate an alternate vet ahead of time removed any chance he had for survival. Please don't make my mistake.

rabbits, analgesia, anesthesia, and therapeutics •

One of the reasons rabbits have been thought of as fragile, difficult-to-treat patients by veterinarians is that the methods of treatment and the medications used were chosen based on what worked for other mammals and were not always appropriate for rabbits. Today veterinarians have access to many rabbit-safe choices, and the rabbit owner who must take his rabbit to the veterinarian is much more likely to take it home again after successful treatment than he was just 10 or 15 years ago. (Provided, of course, the owner has a rabbit-savvy veterinarian familiar with the advances in treating rabbits.)

Analgesia

Rabbits do not tolerate acute or chronic pain well. The stress the rabbit is under from either type of pain can cause its gastrointestinal system to shut down, cause life-threatening gastric ulcers, damage to the kidneys, a dangerous drop in body temperature, and damage to the heart. For this reason, analgesia, or the relief of pain, is of critical importance in treating a rabbit. Unfortunately, researchers have found vets are less likely to use analgesia for rabbits than other companion mammals. If you suspect your rabbit is in pain, ask for an analgesic. Veterinarians experienced with rabbits have found that rabbits given pain relief recover faster, eat sooner, and have fewer gastrointestinal complications.

It is more difficult to recognize pain in rabbits than in many other mammals because the signs are not as obvious. This relates back to the fact that rabbits are prey and must avoid calling attention to themselves. Therefore, the signs of pain are more subtle than in cats or dogs. A rabbit in pain may sit hunched up, be reluctant to move, grind his teeth, breathe from his mouth instead of his nose, flinch at your touch, and/or refuse to eat. Some of the conditions which cause acute or chronic pain in rabbits, and for which they may need to be given pain relief, are gastrointestinal diseases, dental problems, cancer, urolithiasis, arthritis, and trauma such as a broken back or limb.

In general, analgesics safe for other companion mammals are safe for rabbits in lower dosages. Torbugesic® (butorphanol) is an opoid analgesic (narcotic) that is used with success in rabbits. Buprenorphine is also rabbit-safe. Non-steroidal anti-inflammatory (NSAID) analgesics that work well on rabbits are Banamine® (flunixin meglumine) and Metacam®. Rimadyl® (carprofen) is effective for joint and bone pain. Chewable baby aspirin is also used to relieve pain in rabbits.

Anesthesia

Anesthesia involves a loss of *sensation*, pleasurable as well as painful. Owners will be most familiar with anesthesia being used for surgical procedures, although it may also be used during examinations and for sample collection. Local anesthesia removes sensation from a small area and is injected or applied topically. General anesthesia causes a loss of consciousness. A third kind of anesthesia, regional, is rarely used on rabbits. There are risks any time anesthesia is used, particularly general anesthesia.

For many vets, isoflurane gas is the current general anesthetic of choice for rabbits. Although there are some risks using gas anesthesia because it can provoke breath-holding in rabbits, the carefully monitored use of isoflurane gas has greatly improved the rabbit's chances of surviving surgery.

Therapeutics

One of the things that kept rabbit medicine lagging behind that of other companion animals was the lack of knowledge about rabbit-safe therapeutics, especially antibiotics. Antibiotics have a great potential to disrupt the delicate balance of bacteria in the rabbit's cecum, allowing harmful bacteria to gain ascendance. This may not be immediately apparent, as it will most likely take a few days for the effects of a digestive problem to become obvious in the ill rabbit. Your vet should stick to rabbit-safe antibiotics, e.g., fluroquinolones such as enrofloxacin (Baytril®) and marbofloxacin (Marbocyl®), tetracyclines such as doxycyline (Vibramycin®) and oxy-tetracycline, sulphonamides, and chloramphenicol. A combination of sulfadiazine and trimethoprim (Tribrissen®) has also proven successful for treating some bacterial infections in rabbits. As stated earlier, lincomycin, clindamycin, ampicillin, clavamox, and amoxicillin should never be used on rabbits. For those illnesses where it is necessary to use penicillin, the injectable penicillin procaine G with benzathine can be used to safely treat rabbits.

Safe antiparasitic agents include ivermectin and benzimidazoles (thiabendazole, fenbendazole, oxyfenbendazole).

Intestinal motility drugs used with success in rabbits include metoclopramide (Reglan®) for the upper GI tract and cisapride (Propulsid®) for the lower.

caring for rabbits recovering from surgery or illness

The three most important things to remember with a rabbit recovering from surgery or illness are: 1) pain control, 2) cleanliness, 3) love.

Monitor your rabbit for signs of pain. If you suspect your rabbit is suffering too much pain, call your vet and ask for an analgesic. Do what you can to make the rabbit's environment more comfortable. Some rabbits like a soft towel or pillow to lie on when they are recovering. If the rabbit has mouth ulcers, abscesses, or dental problems, pain may prevent it from eating or drinking. Try chopping fresh vegetables into small pieces to make them easier to consume. One of my rabbits had sores in his mouth from dental problems and would not drink. After 12 hours I decided to give him liquid with a syringe, and sat on the floor with a filled syringe balanced over a cup of water. As I picked up a towel and arranged it over my lap so I could hold my rabbit, he took care of the problem by knocking the syringe off the cup and drinking directly from the cup! The sores in his mouth were simply making it too painful for him to drink from his sipper bottle.

Cleanliness is always important when caring for rabbits, and this is doubly true when they are recovering from illness or surgery. Keep the rabbit and the rabbit's cage clean and dry. If the rabbit has diarrhea this is especially important. The cage should be cleaned with white vinegar, and the rabbit can be cleaned with soft cloths dampened with warm water. If the rabbit has long fur, the area around the anus can be trimmed to minimize soiling. Rabbits with urinary incontinence can be fitted with diapers if their incontinence causes hutch burn or other problems (see Chapter 9).

Finally, love and attention are critical to your rabbit's recovery. Rabbits are social animals and do best when lavished with attention. There is a great deal of anecdotal evidence from veterinarians and rabbit owners alike that rabbits given a great deal of care and affection recover better than those which do not. Sometimes just sitting nearby a rabbit recovering from illness or surgery will comfort the rabbit and help it to maintain its will to live. Talk to it quietly and reassuringly. If your rabbit is bonded to other rabbits in your household, don't separate them unless it is necessary because of the nature of the illness. The stress from being separated added to the stress of the illness or surgery itself can prove too much for a rabbit.

Mother Flemish Giant with young. Rabbits are very affectionate animals.

After Surgery

Rabbits recovering from surgery or illness can display widely varying behavior. One may huddle in a corner of the cage, refusing to eat, looking at you with reproachful eyes, and flinching away from your touch. Another may come home from the veterinarian with a good appetite and in no apparent discomfort. Or the rabbit may fall somewhere in between, moving around a little and eating only if coaxed. Two bonded does I had spayed the same day displayed completely different reactions. My Dutch was active, had a good appetite for her usual food, and left her incisions alone. My Holland Lop crouched miserably in a corner of her cage, had to be coaxed to eat a few rolled oats and an oyster cracker, and frequently licked and bit at her incision. Both recovered fully with no complications.

After you bring your rabbit home from the veterinarian's and get him settled, stroke him, talk to him, and be sure he has comfortable, clean bedding at all times. If your rabbit doesn't want to eat when you bring him home after surgery, first coax him with any favored treats. Try a sprig of parsley or cilantro, chopped carrots, an oyster cracker, toasted whole-wheat or seven-grain bread (even white bread if it does the trick). Just getting something in the rabbit's digestive tract is more important than what it is.

If after 24 hours you have been unable to coax your rabbit to eat anything, you will have to force-feed him (also called syringe feeding). Canned pumpkin or a baby food jar of strained carrots with a teaspoon of alfalfa powder mixed in is a good choice for force-feeding. If you don't have baby food, you can cook carrots, cool them, and run them in a blender. The rabbit's regular pellets can also be used for syringe feeding. Grind them in a blender or coffee grinder and add enough water added to make a soupy mixture. There are also commercial syringe feeding formulas available. Oxbow makes one called Critical Care™ that contains an appetite stimulant. It is available through your veterinarian.

When you have the food prepared, fill a 10 cc (small rabbits) or 20 cc (larger rabbits) plastic syringe with it, stick it carefully into the side of the rabbit's mouth, and squeeze in about 2 cc. After the rabbit swallows the first mouthful, repeat the process until he has eaten the full amount. Repeat this three times a day.

Although some rabbits don't mind being syringe fed and will even cooperate, others find it stressful. If your rabbit is one of the latter, you will need to balance the rabbit's need for food with the negative effects of the stress. In general, if your rabbit is fairly strong and usually healthy, syringe feeding three times a day will probably be more helpful than not. On the other hand if your rabbit is always of delicate health and gets extremely stressed by syringe feeding you may wish to discuss the situation with your veterinarian or an experienced rabbit caregiver.

Water is also critical for a convalescent rabbit. If your rabbit is not drinking water, it will also have to be given to the rabbit in a syringe (or you will need to have a veterinarian hydrate your rabbit). As with giving food by syringe, remember to squirt it in the side of the rabbit's mouth to keep the rabbit from aspirating any of the contents. Some rabbit owners recommend giving rabbits acidophilus in their water until their appetites return to normal in order to maintain good intestinal flora. Acidophilus is not naturally found in a rabbit's digestive tract, but there is some evidence that it helps restore the environment necessary for naturally occurring beneficial flora.

Don't let rabbits run free too soon after surgery.

Even if they have been accustomed to being out of their cages for hours a day, keep them confined to their cages for about a week after the surgery. You do not want the rabbit to pull stitches loose or incisions open by allowing too much activity too soon.

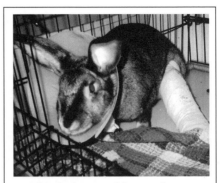

This Satin was able to tolerate an e-collar and a leg cast for over six weeks.

Check any incisions daily for swelling or discharge. Rabbits have a tendency to chew at their stitches, and may irritate the incisions or pull stitches loose. Elizabethan collars are used on cats and dogs to prevent this from happening, but rabbits will rarely tolerate E-collars. The collars may stress rabbits, the rabbit's appetite may fail, and the collar may prevent the rabbit from eating cecotrophs. (Although there are exceptions—my Satin managed to tolerate an E-collar for over two months while a broken hind leg healed. He learned to scoop up food and cecotrophs with the collar!) Keep a close eye on the incisions and call your veterinarian immediately if you notice any discharge or swelling. Bucks that have been neutered may have a little swelling of the scrotum afterward. This is normal, but if the swelling remains past a week you should contact your veterinarian.

If you have had a doe spayed and have a buck at home, keep the buck away from her until she is fully healed, or about a month. A buck who mounts a recently spayed female can injure her. Watch same-sex rabbits and other pets around a rabbit who is recovering from surgery as well. If they become too rough they may need to be kept away from the patient for awhile.

Rabbits Recovering from Illness

Sometimes a rabbit recovering from an illness will have to be isolated from other pets. If this is necessary, it becomes that much more necessary that you spend a great deal of time with the rabbit. A rabbit recovering from illness may not like to be handled, but it often helps the rabbit if you simply sit nearby and talk to him quietly and reassuringly. Be careful to wash your hands after handling a rabbit that is ill, particularly if there are other rabbits in the household.

Keep the rabbit's environment calm and peaceful—no loud TV or rambunctious dogs or children. A rabbit that is ill needs a calm and peaceful place in which to recover. Be sure the temperature is not too hot or cold. If you are accustomed to turning down your heat while you are at work, you might think about leaving it at least on 65 degrees F until your rabbit recovers fully.

If you need to wash wounds or give the rabbit any medications, do so sitting on the floor. If you accidentally cause the rabbit any pain or it simply doesn't like what you're doing, it may kick itself free and injure itself. If you have a great deal of difficulty giving your rabbit medications, try wrapping the rabbit in a towel and holding it in your lap while administering the medication (again, while you are sitting on the floor).

a rabbit emergency kit

It is a good idea to have a rabbit emergency kit in your home. Hopefully you will never need to use it. But if an emergency should arise late at night, on a weekend, a holiday, or any other time when you cannot get immediate veterinary help for your rabbit, having a few emergency supplies on hand may help you keep your rabbit alive until you can get veterinary care. The House Rabbit Resource Network of Austin (address listed in Appendix I) has a relatively inexpensive emergency kit available which I personally have found useful. Or you can put your own together. Most of the necessary items can be bought at a drugstore, and many rabbit supply businesses sell medications, syringes, and other items used for rabbit health care.

Recommended Items for Emergency Kit

Plastic syringes—I recommend having several plastic syringes on hand. Two each of 10 cc (ml), 5 cc, and 1 cc. Syringes with curved tips are useful for hand feeding a rabbit into the side of his mouth and also for bathing wounds with antiseptic.

Towels—A couple of absorbent cotton towels are useful for restraining a rabbit and can also be used for bedding when the rabbit is ill.

Cotton-tipped swabs—These come in handy for applying some medications and also for cleaning rabbit's ears.

List of normal vital signs—In an emergency you may not remember where to find normal ranges for a rabbit's vital signs, so it is a good idea to write them on a slip of paper and put it with the emergency kit, along with your veterinarian's telephone number.

Rectal temperature: 101–103 degrees F (37-39 degrees C)

Heart rate: 130–325 beats per minute (usually about 220 beats per minute).

Respiratory rate: 30–60 breaths per minute.

Thermometer—Either a digital thermometer or an old-style mercury rectal thermometer will work. If you have the latter it may be easier to hold the thermometer in the necessary time if you wrap the rabbit's middle in a towel, confining its legs, and then hold him upside down in your lap while sitting on the floor.

Petroleum jelly—Dabbing a small amount of petroleum jelly on the base of the thermometer before inserting in the rabbit's anus makes it much easier on both rabbit and owner!

Canned pumpkin or strained carrots—It is a good idea to have some canned pumpkin and three or four jars of strained carrots or peas on hand in the event it becomes necessary to syringe feed a rabbit. Some brands of baby foods have lines of organic, additive-free strained vegetables. Do not use baby foods with onion added.

Alfalfa powder—This is usually available at health food

stores. When added to the strained carrots (about one teaspoon to a four-ounce jar), it makes a more complete food for the rabbit.

Acidophilus—Rabbits under stress or receiving antibiotics may need acidophilus to restore their normal intestinal flora. Rabbits given acidophilus do much better, although acidophilus is not normally found in the intestines of a rabbit. Some vets recommend giving rabbits yogurt to accomplish this, but I find my rabbits take acidophilus powder mixed in strained carrots better than they take the yogurt. Acidophilus may also benefit rabbits suffering from ileus.

Electrolyte powder—Electrolyte powder is important if a rabbit is suffering from severe or prolonged diarrhea. If the rabbit won't drink water to which the powder has been added, squirt the mixture into the rabbit's mouth with a syringe.

Simethicone—Intestinal gas in a rabbit can cause severe complications, some of which may result in rapid deterioration and death. Simethicone can be a true life-saver, and is one of the most important items in your emergency kit. It is safe to give rabbits because it acts mechanically, changing the nature of the gas in the rabbit's intestines to make it easier to pass. Break a 125 mg capsule and give half every three hours, then every three to eight hours. Or give a liquid simethicone such as Phazyme®; .5 cc for small rabbits, 1 cc for larger ones. You can repeat the dosage at hour intervals.

Laxatone®, or Petromalt®—These may be of use if your rabbit consumes excessive hair. However, *do not use these preparations if the rabbit is dehydrated.* Some vets believe that in this case the Laxatone® or Petromalt® can actually exacerbate the problem by preventing the hairball from breaking up.

Betadine Solution—This is a good antiseptic wash which is not as traumatic to tissue as hydrogen peroxide and some others.

Chlorahexiderm flush—Antiseptic, antimicrobial with drying properties; useful for cleansing and flushing abscesses. This can also be used for cleaning urine-soaked fur. Note: My veterinarian tells me that betadine and chlorahexiderm are most effective against bacteria when they are diluted with water at a ratio of one part antiseptic to 32 parts water.

Styptic Powder—Use to stop bleeding from a nail which has been cut too short, applying with a cotton-tipped swab. Flour or cornstarch will also work to stop nails from bleeding.

There are various other items that could come in handy in an emergency kit, including gauze bandages, scissors, 81 mg chewable children's aspirin, a tube of original Neosporin® (do not use Neosporin Plus®) or silver sulfadiazine ointment for minor wounds, Gentocin® eye drops or ointment for minor eye irritation, a syringe feeding formula such as Critical Care™, a heating pad, an inexpensive stethoscope for listening to your rabbit's digestive system, and bag balm for abrasions, irritated skin, and sore hocks.

I do not recommend having antibiotics in a home emergency kit. Rabbits' digestive tracts need to maintain a very delicate balance of "good" bacteria to function properly, and antibiotics can disrupt this balance. A veterinarian will take several factors into consideration in determining the proper dosage of antibiotics for your rabbit so that disruption to this balance is minimized. Do not administer antibiotics except under the supervision of a veterinarian.

symptoms of disease

rabbits, if fed correctly, kept clean, and given enough attention and exercise, are remarkably healthy and trouble-free animals despite their seeming fragility. However, like all mammals, there are certain diseases and conditions to which they are susceptible. It is important that the rabbit owner learn the symptoms of common illnesses and be able to recognize when the rabbit is in need of medical attention.

Clinical signs, or symptoms, you might see in your rabbit may be associated with one or more diseases or other medical conditions. Following is a list of symptoms you might notice in your rabbit and some of the conditions and diseases that could cause the symptom. The diseases themselves, along with their other symptoms, causes, and treatment, are listed in Chapter 12.

symptoms and definitions

Abscesses—Collections of pus surrounded by inflamed tissue. In rabbits these often occur on the head or legs, but they may also be found on the rest of the body. Abscesses can also occur on internal organs. Abscesses may be found in rabbits with tularemia, malocclusion, tooth infection, wounds, and pasteurellosis.

Alopecia—Loss of hair. Causes may range from behavioral to parasite infestation or bacterial infections. Pregnant does pull hair from their chest for their nests, and may exhibit this behavior during false pregnancies as well. Another common cause of fur pulling is maloccluded teeth. Infestations of ear mites, fur mites, scabies, fly larvae, and ringworm may result in localized areas of hair loss. Wet dewlap may sometimes be accompanied by hair loss.

Anorexia—Loss of appetite. This is a common symptom of a wide variety of diseases and conditions in rabbits. It may occur as a result of an abrupt diet change, a diet too low in fiber and high in calcium, mouth infections, age, maloccluded teeth, hairballs or other gastrointestinal obstructions, intestinal or hepatic coccidiosis, salmonellosis, Tyzzer's disease, tularemia, myxomatosis, ileus, mucoid enteropathy, acute bloat, volvulus, encephalitozoonosis, mycotoxicosis, rabbit hemorrhagic disease (RHD), myiasis, sore hocks, abscesses, arteriosclerosis, respiratory infections such as pneumonia, ear infections, bladder and kidney infections, urolithiasis, uterine infections, lead poisoning, and heat stress.

Constipation—Small droppings or no droppings. A reduction in the size or amount of your rabbit's droppings should never be ignored. It can be a symptom of a broken back, ileus, acute bloat, volvulus, hairballs or other obstruction of the intestinal tract. If your rabbit produces no droppings for 48 hours, consult your veterinarian.

Convulsions—Rabbits suffering from toxoplasmosis, RHD, arteriosclerosis, encephalitozoonosis, and heat prostration may go into convulsions.

Coughing—Coughing may be seen in rabbits with allergies, and also in rabbits suffering from snuffles.

Dehydration—Dehydration can occur with giardiasis, intestinal coccidiosis, Tyzzer's disease, ileus, volvulus, and mucoid enteropathy. Caution—dehydration in rabbits can be difficult to recognize. See entry this chapter under Emergency First Aid for Rabbits.

Depression—Rabbit is not as active as usual, fails to respond to his environment as usual. This is more pronounced than lethargy. Depression may be a symptom of myiasis, salmonellosis, tularemia, lead or other heavy-metal poisoning, Tyzzer's disease, acute bloat, mucoid enteropathy, urolithiasis, encephalitozoonosis, and snuffles.

Dermatitis—Inflammation of the skin. Skin may be reddened, swollen, crusty or scabby, and there may be hair loss. Dermatitis may be caused by infestations of ear mites, fur mites, scabies, and fleas, or by ringworm, sore hocks, wet dewlap, urine burn, and drooling from maloccluded teeth.

Diarrhea—True diarrhea is uncommon in rabbits, but soft stools are a common symptom you will probably see at one time or another in your rabbit. They can be the result of something as simple as a change of food or too many greens. True diarrhea can be a sign of a life-threatening disease such as colibacillosis. If your rabbit has soft stools, look for other symptoms of disease. If you don't notice any, try feeding your rabbit more hay and fewer fresh vegetables for a few days. It may be caused by diet. If the diarrhea continues, or if it is runny and watery or has blood in it, *seek veterinary help*. In addition to the above, diarrhea can be a symptom of a food allergy, giardiasis, salmonellosis, clostridiosis, intestinal and hepatic coccidiosis.

Diarrhea, bloody—Bloody diarrhea may be seen in rabbits with intestinal coccidiosis.

Diarrhea, mucinous—Diarrhea with mucous can be seen in rabbits suffering from intestinal coccidiosis, mycotoxicosis, and mucoid enteropathy.

Diarrhea, watery—Watery diarrhea may occur in rabbits with intestinal coccidiosis and Tyzzer's disease.

Drooling (ptyalism)—Causes include malocclusion, heat stress, and abdominal pain.

Edema (swelling)—Swelling of the genitals may occur in rabbits suffering from myxomatosis, rabbit pox, and hutch burn. Rabbits with arthritis may exhibit swelling of the affected joints. Swelling of the lips, eyelids, and base of the ears is seen in rabbits with myxomatosis. For swelling of the abdomen see "enlarged abdomen" below.

Enlarged abdomen—In rabbits, usually due to excessive

gas (bloat). Gas may be obstructed by a hairball or other foreign body, or accumulate because of ileus, twisting of intestine (volvulus), intestinal and hepatic coccidiosis, clostridiosis, mucoid enteropathy, and mycotoxicosis.

Epiphora—See "tearing."

Falling—Rabbit falls when he tries to walk. This is seen in rabbits with raccoon and skunk roundworm, and in rabbits suffering from encephalitozoonosis.

Fever (pyrexia)—Temperatures above 104 degrees F (40 degrees C) may be a symptom of cryptosporidiosis, toxoplasmosis, pneumonia, salmonellosis, tularemia, myxomatosis, RHD, heat stroke, toxoplasmosis, and rabbit pox.

Head Shaking—Ear mites, rarely ear infection.

Head Tilt—See "wry neck."

Incontinence, fecal—Broken back.

Incontinence, urinary—Failure to control urine release. This may be exhibited as dribbling as well as total loss of control. May be a symptom of a broken back, toxoplasmosis, urolithiasis, bladder infection, or encephalitozoonosis.

Incoordination—Lack of coordination. This may be a symptom of spinal injury or injury to the limbs, encephalitozoonosis, poisoning, enterotoxemia, heat exhaustion, arthritis, and arteriosclerosis.

Labored breathing—Rabbits suffering from snuffles, pneumonia, RHD, heat stress, and myxomatosis may have labored breathing.

Lethargy—Laziness, indifference, unusual drowsiness. Lethargy may be exhibited in rabbits suffering from giardiasis, clostridiosis, myxomatosis, hairballs, lead poisoning, heat exhaustion, arteriosclerosis, broken back, hepatic coccidiosis, Tyzzer's disease, pneumonia, snuffles, RHD, ileus, raccoon and skunk roundworm.

Low body temperature (hypothermia)—Low body temperature (below 100 degrees F or 37.7 degrees C) is found in rabbits suffering shock after surgery, and can be a symptom of giardiasis, acute bloat, ileus, mucoid enteropathy, and mycotoxicosis.

Nasal discharge—This may be a symptom of snuffles, heat stress, allergies, myxomatosis, RHD, and rabbit pox.

Neoplasm—Tumor.

Ocular discharge—Discharge from the eyes may be caused by dust or a foreign object in the eye, a corneal scratch, allergies, rabbit pox, snuffles, myxomatosis, tooth infections, and bacterial infections of the eye. Rabbits have only one tear duct in an eye, and if the duct is blocked it will cause the eye to run.

Pain—Pain, as evidenced by tooth grinding and sitting in a hunched up position, can be a symptom of several diseases and conditions, including mycotoxicosis, acute bloat, volvulus, mucoid enteropathy, and urolithiasis.

Paralysis—Paralysis can occur as a result of severe malnutrition, fracture of the spine, mycotoxicosis, toxoplasmosis, splayleg, arthritis, encephalitozoonosis, raccoon and skunk roundworm.

Polydipsia (excessive water intake)—This can be caused by heat stress, too much dry feed, enteritis, mucoid enteropathy, hairballs, encephalitozoonosis, and diabetes mellitus. (Normal water intake for rabbits is approximately 100 ml/kg of body weight.)

Pyrexia—See "fever."

Rough coat—Ruffled, dull-looking coats may be found in rabbits suffering from hepatic coccidiosis, clostridiosis, tularemia, myxomatosis, and mycotoxicosis.

Runny eyes—See "ocular discharge."

Scratching—Excessive scratching may be caused by ringworm, ear mites, fur mites, scabies, fleas, or myiasis.

Sneezing—Sneezing is often a symptom of snuffles, but may also be caused by dust, fumes, or allergies.

Sores—See "ulcers."

Swelling—See "edema."

Tearing—See "ocular discharge."

Tremors—May be a symptom of raccoon or skunk roundworm, mycotoxicosis.

Ulcers—Sores in the mouth can be caused by maloccluded teeth or mycotoxicosis. Ulcerated genitals may occur with treponematosis, rabbit pox, or hutch burn. Sores may also be found on the heads and backs of rabbits suffering from scabies, fur mites, sore hocks, and ear mites. Ulcers on the feet are found in rabbits with sore hocks and hutch burn.

Urine, bloody—The first thing that needs to be determined if you see red urine is whether it is caused by blood or is simply red pigmented urine. Sometimes you can tell by the shade of red. Blood in the urine will sometimes look pinkish rather than red, while red pigmented urine may have more of an orange tint. Blood in the urine is often a result of urolithiasis. In female rabbits, urine may sometimes also appear to be bloody when in fact the blood is from a bloody vaginal discharge. If the red color is in the center of a puddle of urine, it is probably blood from the vagina.

Urine, creamy—Whitish urine with sand-like particles.

Urine sand—Crystals, usually of calcium carbonate, appearing in the urine as sand-like particles. A few particles are normal in rabbit urine, but excessive amounts may be sign of excessive calcium in the diet and may be a factor in urolithiasis (see Chapter 12).

Urine sludge—See previous entry.

Vaginal discharge—May be a sign of cancer of the uterus or a genital infection.

Warts—Small whitish warts in the mouth are a sign of infection with oral papillomatosis. Large horny warts on the head or body are a symptom of infection by the Shope papilloma virus.

Weepy eye—See "ocular discharge."

Weight loss—This symptom may not necessarily occur in association with loss of appetite. Causes include malocclusion, hairball, nutrient deficiency, snuffles, giardiasis, encephalitozoonosis, arteriosclerosis, a tumor, hepatic coccidiosis, sore hocks, lead or other heavy-metal poisoning, mycotoxicosis, and urolithiasis.

Wry neck (torticollis)—Head tilt. This can be a symptom of a bacterial infection (usually *Pasteurella*) which has spread to the middle or inner ear or brain. It can also be caused by a severe ear mite infestation, encephalitozoonosis, head injuries, and raccoon or skunk roundworm.

monthly check-up

Once a month you should check your rabbit's general condition and look for any of the above symptoms. It just takes a few minutes after the first three or four times, and may be the means of catching a potentially serious health problem while it can still be treated easily.

183

Begin by running your hands over the rabbit from head to rump, feeling for any lumps or lesions. Look at the condition of the fur: it should be shiny and not have any dandruff-like particles. Rub the rabbit's jaws (avoiding under the chin, which is a ticklish spot for most rabbits), feeling carefully for any small lumps, and noticing the rabbit's reaction. If he jerks back or exhibits discomfort, it may be the sign of an infected tooth root or abscess. Check the incisors for excessive length and curvature, which can be signs of malocclusion.

Taking the time to give your rabbit a monthly check-up will help keep it healthy and perky like this female Dutch.

Look at the rabbit's eyes. They should be clear and bright, with no excessive discharge. Some accumulation of dried mucous is normal. If you wish, you can wipe it away with a clean finger or cotton swab. Watch for excessive wetness around the eyes or an extremely runny eye. Excessive tearing is not uncommon in rabbits because rabbits' eyes only have one tear duct and it can become blocked fairly easily (as with dried mucous). Normally it will clear up within a day or so, but if an eye continues to tear badly the condition should be watched. It can be a sign of a more serious condition (see "ocular discharge" entry earlier in this chapter). Also check the eyes for redness, spots, and clouding. Should any of these conditions be present and persist for several days, have the rabbit checked by a veterinarian. The nictitating membrane (third eyelid) should not be up. If it is, check the bunny carefully for any other symptoms of ill health.

Now check the inside of the ears for any signs of mites or excessive wax and dirt build-up. This is especially important with lops. If they are too dirty, it will be necessary to either clean them out yourself (gently!) with cotton moistened with hydrogen peroxide or ask your veterinarian to do it for you.

Next turn the rabbit upside down in your lap and check its nails and the bottoms of the hind feet. If the nails are getting too long and tearing or bleeding, you will need to clip them or have it done at your veterinarian's. If the bottoms of the hind feet show any bald spots, you will have to take action to prevent the rabbit from developing ulcers on his feet (see "sore hocks," Chapter 12). If sores have already developed, you will need to take your rabbit to a veterinarian for treatment.

While you have the rabbit upside down in your lap check the genital area. Is there any feces matted on the fur that could indicate a diet too high in protein or a gastrointestinal problem? Are the genitals swollen or scabby? Does the skin appear reddened or irritated (signs of possible urinary trouble)? If you detect a strong, almost skunk-like odor while you are holding your rabbit upside down, the inguinal gland area may need cleaning. These glands are located on either side of the genitals and sometimes get a wax-like, dirty build-up. If they appear brownish you will need to take a cotton swab moistened with hydrogen peroxide and clean them off.

Lastly, look at your rabbit as he hops away after the exam. Does he show any difficulty hopping? Does he hold his head at a tilt? If not, and you have found no other problems during your exam, your rabbit is probably in pretty good health.

"help, my bunny . . ."

Sometimes new rabbit owners see things in their rabbit they aren't sure are normal or not. In this section are a few of the things rabbit owners may notice and wonder about. Actual first aid treatment for serious conditions is listed in the following section.

"Help, my bunny's . . .

abdomen is swollen." This may be a sign of severe gas or acute bloat and must be treated *immediately* with simethicone to save the rabbit's life. See entry for severe gas/acute bloat under emergency first aid for rabbits.

coughing/choking." Rabbits may occasionally cough, choke, and/or snort when they are eating and drinking and get water or dust from hay or pellets up their nostrils. This is especially common with lops. Most likely the rabbit will stop within a minute or two. You can take a clean soft cloth and gently wipe the nostrils. If the coughing/choking should continue for more than a few minutes, consult a veterinarian.

crouched in the back of his cage doing nothing." If the rabbit's posture is tense, if he is grinding his teeth, and/or he has a swollen abdomen, he may be in severe pain from bloat or another serious condition. See the entries for severe gas and acute bloat under emergency first aid for rabbits.

diarrhea is bad." Be sure it is truly diarrhea and not just smashed cecotrophs. A rabbit given a too-rich diet may produce excessive cecotrophs which become smashed and smeared under his feet. See entry for diarrhea under emergency first aid for rabbits.

ears are hot." Rabbits' ears are one of the means by which heat is regulated in their bodies. They may at times feel quite hot or cold. Normally this is nothing to worry about.

eyes are runny." The technical term for this is epiphora. It is most likely caused by a temporary irritation from hay or pellet dust, or a scratched cornea. Wipe the fur around the eyes to prevent it from getting too wet. You can also flush the rabbit's eye with a commercial solution. Should the problem continue for more than a day or two, consult a vet. See entry for "ocular discharge" under symptoms and definitions at the start of this chapter.

falling down when he tries to walk." If your rabbit falls when he tries to walk, but does not appear to have a broken limb, he may be suffering from a serious disease or poisoning. Get your rabbit to a veterinarian as soon as possible.

head is tilting sideways." This should always be checked out by a vet, as it could be a sign of an ear infection or more serious disease. See entry for head tilt under emergency first aid for rabbits.

hiccoughing." Three of my rabbits occasionally hiccough. It never continues very long, and does not appear to cause any problems. Leave your rabbit alone and it should stop soon. If the hiccoughing should continue more than a few minutes, consult a veterinarian.

leg is dangling." Most likely the leg is broken. If both legs are limp and rabbit cannot walk or is dragging his hind legs, the rabbit probably has a broken back. See entry for broken bones under emergency first aid for rabbits.

lying on the floor not moving." Most likely your rabbit is just sleeping. Sometimes, especially when they lie on their side with legs stiffly extended, it can look frightening, but most likely nothing is wrong. However, if it is

It takes time to learn what is normal behavior for a rabbit.

especially hot or humid and your rabbit is also gasping or breathing very rapidly, he may be suffering from heat stress. See the entry for heat exhaustion in Chapter 12.

making strange noises." Try to pin down the noise. Is it grunting, humming, spitting, or tooth grinding? A soft grunting or humming noise may simply be the sounds of a happy and contented rabbit. A loud grunting or spitting may indicate an angry or frightened rabbit. A very soft tooth grinding is a rabbit's way of purring. But a loud tooth grinding or tooth gnashing is a sign of severe pain. Check your rabbit to see if he has any other signs of a serious problem, such as an enlarged abdomen, and get him to a vet promptly.

nail is bleeding all over the place." Occasionally a rabbit's nail may tear, or we may accidentally cut too far when trimming a nail, causing it to bleed. Although it seems like a lot of blood, don't panic. Press some flour or styptic powder onto the end of the nail and put him into his cage where he will feel safe. It should stop bleeding within a few minutes.

not eating/drinking." The key here is the amount of time that goes by. If it's only been a couple of hours, likely the rabbit is just full, a little stressed, or possibly too warm. But if a day passes without a rabbit eating or drinking or if is accompanied by other symptoms such as a swollen abdomen or crouching and tooth gnashing, the rabbit may have a serious gastrointestinal condition, dental problem, or other disease. See the entries under gastrointestinal conditions, malocclusion, and heat exhaustion in Chapter 12.

not producing feces." Again, the key is how long the condition has continued. A rabbit does not produce feces continually throughout the day (although it may seem that way sometimes). But if several hours pass without the rabbit producing feces, or if you see little tiny feces, it may be a sign of a gastrointestinal problem. See the entries under gastrointestinal conditions in Chapter 12.

scratching his ears/shaking his head." All rabbits will occasionally scratch their ears or shake their heads. But if your rabbit does this excessively, it could be a sign of wax build-up, an ear infection, or ear mites. If your rabbit is a lop, it is most likely an excessive build-up of wax and debris. Ear mites are also a common cause of head shaking. Or it could be an early sign of an ear infection. Take your rabbit to a vet to find out.

urine is red/orange." Most likely the rabbit's urine is red or orange because of the foods he has been eating. This is nothing to worry about. A pinkish tinge to the urine, or a reddish/pinkish spot in the middle of a puddle of urine, is probably blood. If you think you see blood in your rabbit's urine, take him a veterinarian.

emergency first aid for rabbits

We all hope it does not happen to us, but emergencies can arise when we must depend upon ourselves to keep our rabbit alive long enough to get him to a veterinarian. Situations that might require us to do this are when the rabbit becomes unconscious, gasps for air, has seizures, severe diarrhea, uncontrolled bleeding, or shows evidence of acute bloat or a broken bone. Other emergency situations may not be as obvious, as when a rabbit has not eaten for 24 hours, is not producing feces, is unable to urinate, or is severely dehydrated.

If you suspect you have an emergency situation, take the rabbit's temperature if you can do so without causing him further injury. If the rabbit's temperature is lower than 100 degrees F, you will need to try and warm him slightly. Use a heating pad set on low heat, or fill a water bottle or other container with warm water, wrap it in a cloth, and place it next to the rabbit. If the rabbit's temperature is over 104 degrees F, you can wrap him in a towel dampened in *tepid* water.

In any emergency situation, watch the rabbit for signs of shock. This is easiest to spot through the color of the rabbit's gums. If they are brighter pink than usual, or if they turn grayish or white, the rabbit is in shock. Getting the rabbit to a veterinarian is critical if there are any signs of shock.

Artificial Respiration of Rabbits

Be *very* sure the rabbit is not breathing before you attempt this, or you might harm him. Wet your fingers and put them in front of his nose to feel for any breath, or try holding a small mirror just before his nostrils and see if any moisture becomes apparent on the mirror.

If your rabbit is not breathing, there are two methods of artificial respiration.

1) Dr. Anne Downes, in the winter 2000 issue of *The Bunny Thymes,* describes a method of artificial respiration for rabbits developed by Dr. Thomas Donnelly: Hold the rabbit's forelimbs in one hand, the hind limbs in the other, extend the rabbit in the air horizontally, and rock

191

the rabbit head-up to head-down every two seconds.

2) For the traditional method of artificial respiration, cover the rabbit's nose and mouth with your mouth and breathe out a gentle puff of air. Repeat every five seconds.

If there is no response after five minutes with either method, cease.

Difficulty Breathing

Check the nose for blockage by mucous. If there is dried mucous blocking the nasal passages, clean it gently away with a soft damp cloth. Rarely, an object such as a blade of hay may get up a rabbit's nose and cause it to have difficulty breathing. If such an object can easily be seen and removed, do so. If you can see something in the bunny's nostril but don't think you can remove it without harming him, take him to a vet.

If the rabbit is raising his head and gasping, he may have heat stroke. If the room temperature is above 85 degrees F and the rabbit's rectal temperature is above 104 degrees F, immerse the rabbit in *tepid* water (not cool or cold water) for about three minutes and then get him to a vet as fast as possible.

Severe Bleeding

Apply direct pressure with an absorbent gauze pad until the bleeding slows. If the pad soaks through, do not remove it, but keep adding fresh ones on top of the old ones. When the bleeding slows enough to allow you to release the pressure, secure the pad(s) in place and get the rabbit to a vet. Bleeding from nails (although it appears bad) will usually stop by itself within a few minutes. Put flour or styptic powder on the bleeding nail to slow flow of blood.

Broken Bones

If the rabbit is dragging both hind limbs it probably has a broken back. Wrap him carefully in a towel (being sure the spine is in a natural position and not twisted) and take him to a veterinarian.

If only one leg is dangling, the injury is most likely a broken limb. You can try to splint it with a pencil or stick and soft bandage, although if it is a rear limb this may not be possible. Restrict the rabbit's movement by putting him in a small cage or box. If pieces of the bone are protruding through the skin and/or there is bleeding accompanying the dangling limb, it is particularly important to get the rabbit to a veterinarian as soon as possible.

Veterinarians who are not experienced treating rabbits or who are not up-to-date on current developments in rabbit medicine may recommend euthanasia of rabbits with broken backs or limbs. This has happened to me. Get a second opinion before making any decision. Broken limbs can often be mended successfully. If saving the limb is not possible, rabbits can do well as amputees. Rabbits with broken backs can sometimes lead quality lives with devoted care and a specially fitted cart.

Convulsions

Convulsions will usually stop within two minutes. Clear the area so the rabbit does not hurt himself. When the convulsions stop, get him to the vet. If the convulsions do not stop within five minutes, put him into a box well-padded with towels and take him to a vet immediately.

Diarrhea

Any diarrhea is a cause for concern, but severe diarrhea will require administration of subcutaneous fluids as well as medications to treat the cause. Take a rabbit suffering from severe diarrhea to a veterinarian as soon as possible. For less severe diarrhea, see entry under "diarrhea" earlier in this chapter.

Beginning rabbit caregivers, do not confuse a rabbit's "night droppings" (see Chapter 6) with diarrhea. If a rabbit does not consume all his night dropping, they can become smeared and appeared to be minor diarrhea.

Failure to Eat or Drink

Rabbits in pain from illness or injury will often quit eating and drinking. If your rabbit has not eaten for over 24 hours, it will be necessary to force-feed him with a syringe (see Chapter 10). Water can be given the same way. However, if the stomach appears to be full (as can happen if there is a gastrointestinal obstruction), caution should be observed in administering fluids orally. The rabbit should be taken to a veterinarian so fluids can be given subcutaneously. Severe dehydration will probably also necessitate administration of subcutaneous fluids.

Caution: Some veterinarians warn (and I have found this to be true in my own experience) that dehydration is not as easy to test in a rabbit as it is in a cat. "Tenting" the skin the way one does with a cat may not work with rabbits—a dehydrated rabbit's skin may appear normal because a rabbit's physiology is such that water will be taken from the intestines to maintain hydration of the rest of the body. This will cause the rabbit's feces to be dry or cause production to cease. If feces are dry and feces production slows or ceases, your rabbit may be severely dehydrated.

Severe Gas and Acute Bloat

Any signs of severe gas (enlarged abdomen, failure to defecate, subnormal temperature, loud gurgling from the rabbit's stomach, signs of severe pain such as teeth grinding or sitting in a hunched up position) should be treated *immediately*. Give the rabbit half of a 125 mg capsule of simethicone or a dose of liquid simethicone (.5 cc for smaller rabbits, 1 cc for larger ones), and repeat every hour. Apply external heat (heating pad set on low or hot water bottle filled with warm water and wrapped in a cloth). If the rabbit shows signs of being in severe pain, give it half a tablet of children's' 81 mg chewable aspirin. Acute bloat can come on very rapidly, and if it is not treated, the rabbit can die in less than 24 hours.

The following chart lists only a few of the many diseases and conditions that may affect rabbits. Its purpose is to help rabbit owners get a picture of what symptoms may occur with what diseases. Please use it with caution and do not rely upon the chart for a diagnosis of your pet. The chart is necessarily simplified, and a veterinarian will take many other factors into consideration when making a diagnosis.

C = A symptom that is commonly associated with a disease or condition, but not always.
M = A major symptom that is almost always associated with the disease or condition.
O = An occasional symptom that may or may not occur with a disease or condition.

	ear mites	fly strike (myiasis)	fur mites	intestinal coccidiosis	hepatic coccidiosis	encephalitozoonosis	toxoplasmosis	weepy eye (conjunctivitis)
dermatitis	C		M					
scratching	M	C	M					
hair loss	O	O	C					
rough coat					C			
head shaking	C							
fever							C	
hypothermia								
polydipsia						O		
dehydration				O				
drooling								
anorexia (appetite loss)		O		C	C	O	C	
weight loss	O				C			
diarrhea				C	O			
few or no feces								
sludge in urine								
incontinence						O		
ocular discharge								M
nasal discharge								
labored breathing								
snuffling and sneezing								
enlarged abdomen				O	O			
swollen genitals								
swollen eyes and nose								
ulcerations on genitals	O							
ulcerations in mouth								
paralysis						O	O	
convulsions						O	O	
wry neck	O					O		
depression		O				O		
lethargy					O			
pain, acute								

racoon roundworm	mycotoxicosis	RHD (VHD, RCV)	myxomatosis	tularemia	clostridiosis	snuffles	pneumonia	hairball	ileus (GI stasis)	acute bloat	hutch burn	urolithiasis	heat stress	malocclusion	broken back
														C	
														O	
	C		C	C	C										
			C	M	M		M								
	C								C	M					
							C					C			
								O					O		
												C	C		M
	C	C	M	C	O	O	C	O	C	M		O	C	C	
	C							C				O		C	
			M			C									
		C	C			M									
		O	C										M		
						M									
	O					C		O	C	M					
			C								M				
			C												
											O				
	C													C	
C	O														M
C	O	O										O			
C					O										
				O	C			C		C	O				
C		C			M	C	C	C	O				C		M
	C		C							M		C		O	

Head Tilt (Wry Neck)

The rabbit's head may tilt so far the rabbit has great difficulty hopping, and in some cases the rabbit may fall down and/or the eyes may roll. Prepare a padded box and get the rabbit to a veterinarian as soon as possible. Rabbits with less serious head tilt should also be taken to a veterinarian, as head tilt is usually a symptom of serious disease or infection.

Caution: a veterinarian who is not sufficiently familiar with rabbit medicine may recommend euthanasia of rabbits with head tilt. If this happens to you, get a second opinion. Head tilt is not always a sign of an untreatable disease.

Failure to Urinate

If a rabbit is straining in his litter box and showing signs of pain such as teeth grinding, his urinary tract may be blocked by a stone. This is more common in males, older rabbits, and rabbits that have previously shown signs of excess calcium such as creamy urine or urine sludge. Get the rabbit to a vet promptly.

Wounds

Wash blood off and cleanse with betadine solution. If the wound is particularly deep or was a puncture wound, you should probably take the rabbit to a vet. Minor wounds can be treated with original Neosporin® (not Neosporin Plus®), or silver sulfadiazine ointment. Unpasteurized honey can also be used to help heal wounds. Apply as you would an ointment. Watch any wounds closely for redness, swelling, and any signs of developing infection.

specific diseases and conditions of pet rabbits

the diseases included in this chapter are by no means all that might be found in pet rabbits. I have tried to include those the rabbit owner would be most likely to encounter and others which are less common but which the rabbit owner may have heard of and would wonder about. A few "diseases" that are actually symptoms, e.g., abscesses, are included because of the common usage of the terms to describe a medical condition in a rabbit. Others are cross-referenced: pasteurellosis is listed both under bacterial diseases and under some of the symptoms or conditions it may cause, e.g. head tilt and abscesses. Please do not rely upon the information in this chapter for a definitive diagnosis of what ails your rabbit. Always consult your veterinarian.

mycotic (fungal) conditions

There are relatively few fungi that may affect your rabbit. Perhaps the greatest danger from fungi is mycotoxicosis, or poisoning caused by the ingestion of feedstuffs contaminated by fungi. Ringworm can occur in rabbits, but it usually responds well to treatment.

Mycotoxicosis

<u>Causal agent:</u> Toxins produced by molds.

<u>Symptoms:</u> Ulcers in mouth, anorexia, weight loss, acute bloat, severe pain, rough coat, paralysis, tremors, hypothermia, mucinous feces.

<u>Treatment:</u> Subcutaneous fluids, antibiotics, sucralfate (staggered three to six hours apart from other drugs).

A well-loved and cared for rabbit will most likely live a long and healthy life.

<u>Transmission:</u> Ingestion of contaminated feedstuffs (mycotoxins have been found in alfalfa hay, grass hay, wheat middlings, alfalfa pellets, timothy pellets, and other feeds for rabbits).

<u>Prevention:</u> Feed rabbits only high-quality pellets and hay. Check all hay and feed before giving to rabbits. Hay should be dry, green, and sweet-smelling. Any hay or feed which has gotten damp should be destroyed.

Ringworm *(dermatophytosis)*

<u>Causal agent:</u> *Trichophyton mentagrophytes* var. *granulare, Microsporum canis.*

<u>Symptoms:</u> Scratching; circular, reddened patches on the skin, frequently appearing first on the bridge of the

nose, eyelids, ears, head and then spreading to the rest of the body. It can also be carried asymptomatically.

TREATMENT: Topical antifungal ointments such as enilconazole, oral antifungal medications such as griseofulvin.

TRANSMISSION: This fungus is uncommon in rabbits, but may be contracted by contact with infected guinea pigs, cats, dogs, or humans.

PREVENTION: Keep any other affected pets away from rabbits.

parasites

Wild rabbits are almost always infected with one or several parasites, but domestic rabbits are affected less often. Parasites that may attack pet rabbits range from fleas to warble flies to worms and protozoans.

Ectoparasites: *The following entries include parasites you will find on the body of your rabbit.*

Fleas

CAUSAL AGENT: Many species of fleas, including *Ctenocephalides felis, C. canis, Polex irritans, Cediopsylla simples, Odontopsyllus multispinosus.* In Europe, *Spilopsyllus cuniculi.* Most fleas will infest many different species of hosts.

SYMPTOMS: Scratching, dermatitis, flea dirt visible.

TREATMENT: It was formerly thought that fleas in a rabbit could be safely treated with preparations used for cats. However, veterinarians have reported adverse reactions by rabbits when treated with some of the cat-safe preparations, including Advantage® (imidacloprid) and Frontline® (fipronil). Some vets recommend that any medication containing fipronil not be used. Carbarryl and preparations with pyrethrin have been used successfully on rabbits. Program®, given at dosages of half that for a small cat, seems to work on rabbits. If the rabbit shows any of the following symptoms after treatment for fleas, stop the treatment and contact the vet: tremors, anorexia, dermatitis, scratching, unusual behavior. Never use a flea collar on a rabbit. Rabbits have been known to choke themselves trying to get one off, and materials in the collar may be toxic to the rabbit. Be sure to treat the rabbit's environment for fleas as well.

TRANSMISSION: By contact.

PREVENTION: If other animals in the household are allowed outside, they may bring fleas in to the rabbit. Watch your rabbit closely for signs of infestation if you have dogs or cats in your household that are allowed outside in an area where fleas are common. Fleas can transmit several serious diseases of rabbits, and should never remain untreated.

Fly strike *(myiasis)*

CAUSAL AGENT: Fly larvae, often of greenbottles (*Lucilia* spp.) and bluebottles (*Calliphora* spp.).

SYMPTOMS: Anorexia, restlessness, maggots visible under fur.

TREATMENT: Area must be clipped and cleaned and maggots removed by hand. Rabbit should then be treated with antibiotics and given an analgesic such as carprofen. Some veterinarians recommend ivermectin as a precaution for missed maggots.

TRANSMISSION: Eggs are usually laid around anal area.

PREVENTION: Keep rabbit's bedding clean and dry and clean any matted fur around anal area. Rabbits that are unable to groom themselves properly due to conditions such as malocclusion, obesity, arthritis, and spondylosis are at higher risk.

Fly, warble *(warbles)*

CAUSAL AGENT: Fly larvae of *Cuterebra* spp. (This fly is not found in the U.K.)

SYMPTOMS: Depression, anorexia, scratching, hair loss, raised bump about half an inch in diameter with a small hole in the middle. Larva can be seen if hole is watched.

TREATMENT: Larvae must be removed whole: if larvae are ruptured while in rabbit's skin, rabbit will have severe reaction to released toxins and may die. It is better to have this done by a veterinarian than to attempt it yourself.

TRANSMISSION: Fly lays eggs on rabbit; larvae hatch and then enter the rabbit, often by nose, mouth, or open wounds. Bumps where the larvae create a breathing hole can be found in such places as groin, neck, under the limbs, and on the back and rump.

PREVENTION: Sanitation. Keep rabbit's environment clean and dry so it does not attract flies. Kill any flies which get into the house. Older rabbits are less likely to be affected.

Mites, ear *(ear canker, otoacariasis)*

CAUSAL AGENT: *Psoroptes cuniculi.*

SYMPTOMS: Scratching, shaking head, dermatitis, an accumulation of brown crusty material in the external ear canal. In severe cases ulcerations may be found on the outside of the ears and on top of the head, and there may be spasms of the eye muscles. Severe secondary infections can damage the inner ear and central nervous system, causing wry neck. Rarely, ear mites affect genitalia.

TREATMENT: Ear mites can be treated with mineral oil and miticides used for dogs and cats. The drops should be applied daily in the ear canal, and in a bad case, down the side of the head and neck as well. Injections of ivermectin will also control ear mites. The crusty material may be removed from the ears with cotton soaked in dilute hydrogen peroxide. The rabbit's cage should be well cleaned to prevent reinfestation.

TRANSMISSION: Direct contact.

PREVENTION: Ear mites are highly contagious, and will persist in the environment for several weeks. Sanitation is critical. It is a good idea to have any new rabbit checked for ear mites whether signs of infestation are present or not.

Mites, fur *(skin mange, walking dandruff)*

CAUSAL AGENT: In the U.S., usually *Cheyletiella parasitovorax*. Also *Leporacus gibbus* (formerly *Listrophorus gibbus*), the true fur mite.

SYMPTOMS: Dermatitis, scratching, clumps of hair falling out, small sores and scabs on the neck, dandruff visible in fur. Very light infestations may have no noticeable symptoms.

TREATMENT: Medicated shampoo or injections of ivermectin over a two- to three-week period.

TRANSMISSION: By contact. *Cheyletiella* mites may also bite humans.

PREVENTION: Good sanitation, keeping infected animals away from rabbits.

Scabies *(Mange)*

CAUSAL AGENT: *Sarcoptes scabei* or *Notoedres cati*.

SYMPTOMS: Dermatitis, constant scratching, loss of hair (particularly on face). Secondary infections may occur, causing oozing sores.

TREATMENT: Dipping rabbit in a lime-sulfur preparation. Injections of invermectin three times at two-week intervals.

TRANSMISSION: By contact.

PREVENTION: Scabies is not common in the U.S., but rabbits can become infested through contact with other affected pets or humans. The best prevention is to keep rabbits from affected animals.

Endoparasites: *The following entries include parasites you will be unlikely to see on your rabbit since they attack from within the body. I am separating them into worms and protozoal parasites, the latter which are intracellular parasites.*

Worms

Pinworm

CAUSAL AGENT: *Passalurus ambiguus* (a nematode).

SYMPTOMS: Thread-like worms visible in feces, excessive grooming of anal area.

TREATMENT: Because pinworms rarely cause a rabbit problems even if large numbers are present, they are often not treated unless they are upsetting to the owner. Piperazine citrate added to the rabbit's water can be effective in ridding the rabbit of these worms. Parasiticides such as fenbendazole and oxyfenbendazole have also been used.

TRANSMISSION: Through ingestion of contaminated food and water. Spores are shed in the urine and can remain viable for months. Rabbit pinworms are not transmissible to humans.

PREVENTION: Pinworms are extremely common in rabbits and may be difficult to prevent even with good sanitation.

Roundworm, raccoon

CAUSAL AGENT: *Baylisascaris procyonis.*

SYMPTOMS: Wry neck (head tilt), tremors, lethargy, falling, paralysis, coma and death. These symptoms occur when the worm larvae have migrated into the brain, liver, eyes, spinal cord, or other organs. This condition is almost always fatal to rabbits.

TREATMENT: Corticosteroids can be given to reduce inflammation of tissues. High dosages of oxybendazole given over long periods of time show some promise in slowing the progress of this condition.

TRANSMISSION: Through contamination by raccoon feces of grass, feed or bedding which is then ingested by the rabbit. Raccoon roundworms are also transmissible to humans, and are usually fatal to humans as well. Note— this parasite is only transmissible by raccoons. Other infected mammals cannot transmit the parasite.

PREVENTION: Caution and good sanitation. Because of the danger of this parasite to humans as well as pets, keep all children and pets from raccoon latrine areas. Destroy any bedding or feed contaminated by raccoons, and wear a protective face mask and gloves while doing so. A propane torch can be used to kill eggs in contaminated soil.

Roundworm, skunk

CAUSAL AGENT: *Baylisascaris columnaris.*

SYMPTOMS, TREATMENT, TRANSMISSION, and PREVENTION are the same as for raccoon roundworm, except the carrier is the skunk.

Tapeworm

CAUSAL AGENT: *Cysticercus pisiformis* (larval stage of *Taenia pisiformis*), *Coenurus serialis* (larval stage of *Taenia serialis*), *Echinococcus granulosus, Cittotaenia* spp.

SYMPTOMS: Anorexia, enlarged abdomen, swellings under skin.

TRANSMISSION: Ingestion of feed (especially grass) contaminated with eggs.

PREVENTION: The primary host of most tapeworms that affect rabbits is the dog. Rabbits should not be allowed to eat grass in areas where dogs run. Rabbits are the primary host of *Cittotaenia*, but this tapeworm is usually found in wild rabbits, rarely domestic rabbits.

Protozoal Parasites (Intracellular Parasites)

Coccidiosis, hepatic

CAUSAL AGENT: *Eimeria stiedae* (protozoan).

SYMPTOMS: Mild or no symptoms; sometimes anorexia, rough coat, weight loss, enlarged abdomen, lethargy, diarrhea. In this form of coccidiosis the parasites invade the liver rather than forming colonies on intestine walls. It is more serious than intestinal coccidiosis.

TREATMENT: Sulfaquinoxaline, sulfamethazine. Treatment is only effective during early stages in the life cycle of the parasite—probably before the owner knows the rabbit is affected.

TRANSMISSION: Rabbits become infested by ingesting food or water contaminated with feces containing sporulated oocysts. Oocysts require two days outside the host to sporulate, but then remain viable in soil, caging, feed, etc. for months.

PREVENTION: Good sanitation practices. Ordinary disinfectants do not kill oocysts. Steam is an effective method for disinfecting an area of oocysts.

Coccidiosis, intestinal

CAUSAL AGENT: *Eimeria* spp. (protozoa).

SYMPTOMS: Usually mild or no symptoms; sometimes anorexia, watery diarrhea or blood and/or mucous in feces, dehydration, enlarged abdomen.

TREATMENT: Intestinal coccidosis is more common than hepatic coccidosis, and is rarely fatal. It can be treated with sulfa antibiotics such as sulfaquinoxaline and sulfamethazine. The cage should be cleaned with a 10 percent ammonia solution to kill oocysts.

TRANSMISSION: These protozoa are most often transmitted to the rabbit when the rabbit ingests food or water contaminated with sporulated oocysts. Although coccidia are usually quite host specific, some authors claim there is a possibility rabbits could contract the parasite through contact with rodents, cats, dogs, or birds.

Cryptosporidiosis

CAUSAL AGENT: *Cryptosporidium cuniculus* (protozoan).

SYMPTOMS: No symptoms to fever and death within a few days.

TREATMENT: Parasiticides.

TRANSMISSION: Through ingestion of contaminated feces.

PREVENTION: The rabbit is an intermediate host of this protozoan. Cats are the definitive host. Rabbits in households with cats can potentially jump into the cat's litter box, step in infected cat feces, and then ingest oocysts when cleaning their feet. Rabbit owners who also own cats should be very careful to keep the cat's litter box immaculately clean, to wash their hands after cleaning the litter box, and to keep the rabbits from using it, if possible.

Encephalitozoonosis *(nosematosis)*

CAUSAL AGENT: *Encephalitozoon cuniculi* (protozoal microsporidian). Previously *Nosema cuniculi, E. negri.*

SYMPTOMS: Usually no symptoms or slight symptoms; rarely the following: depression, anorexia, polydipsia, incontinence, wry neck, muscle weakness, paralysis of hindquarters, convulsions, or sudden death. Mainly affects kidneys and central nervous system, although in seriously infected rabbits all tissues can be affected.

TREATMENT: There is currently no drug therapy that cures encephalitozoonosis, although tetracycline, chloramphenicol, albendozole, or oxyfenbendazole have been used to help stabilize the rabbit. Some rabbits recover without treatment.

TRANSMISSION: Aerosol and by ingestion of spore-containing urine, as when feed is contaminated with urine containing infective spores and then consumed. May also be transmitted placentally from doe to kit.

PREVENTION: Good sanitation. Dwarf rabbits appear to be more susceptible than other rabbits. Encephalitozoonosis is only contagious while the parasites are in the kidneys, a three-month period. Unfortunately the owner will probably not know the rabbit has the parasite at this stage. Therefore, good sanitation practices are the best prevention. Rabbit owners with dogs, cats, hamsters, guinea pigs, or birds should be especially attentive to good sanitation practices. Always wash hands after cleaning dog feces from yards, cat litter boxes, and bird cages. Dispose of any rabbit bedding or feed that becomes contaminated with rodent or bird feces.

Giardiasis

CAUSAL AGENT: *Giardia* spp. (protozoa).

SYMPTOMS: Diarrhea, weight loss, dehydration, lethargy, low body temperature.

TREATMENT: This is most often seen in very young rabbits, often those from pet stores. Nutritional supplements, heat, fluids, and parasiticides such as fenbendazole and oxyfenbendazole are used to treat it. The antibiotic Flagyl® (metronidazole) is also sometimes prescribed.

TRANSMISSION: Ingestion of cysts from feces.

PREVENTION: Dispose of all dog and cat feces promptly and wash hands afterwards. Cysts can remain on the hair of dogs and cats and could potentially be a source of infection.

Toxoplasmosis

CAUSAL AGENT: *Toxoplasma gondii* (protozoan).

SYMPTOMS: Fever, convulsions, paralysis, death within a few days.

TREATMENT: This is relatively rare in rabbits, but can occur in households with pet cats.

TRANSMISSION: Through ingestion of cat feces containing infective oocysts.

PREVENTION: Good sanitation.

bacterial diseases

There are several bacteria which commonly infect rabbits, causing a variety of diseases and symptoms. Some of these will be found cross-referenced by body part affected under "Other Diseases and Conditions" later in this chapter.

Abscesses

CAUSAL AGENT: Usually *Pasteurella multocida,* also *Staphylococcus aureus, Pseudomonas, Bacterioides, Proteus.*

SYMPTOMS: This is a case where the name of the condition is the symptom. An abscess is a localized collection of pus with pathogenic organisms, and the owner will notice it as a swelling. In rabbits it will often be seen in the mouth, on the head and legs, or anywhere a rabbit has been bitten or otherwise wounded. Abscesses may also occur on internal organs. The pus in a *P. multocida* abscess in usually thick and creamy-white. Abscesses may be difficult to diagnose. Rabbits may continue to eat well and appear to feel well. Sometimes abscesses may be felt as lumps under the skin; those occurring on the head may cause eye and nose problems.

TREATMENT: Abscesses in rabbits are often difficult to treat successfully. They frequently develop "fingers" that are difficult to clean out and the thick pus is hard to drain. The best treatment is to have a vet remove the abscess surgically and follow with antibiotic therapy. If this is not possible, the vet should prescribe Bicillin® C-R antibiotic therapy. In a promising new treatment, a "bead" containing antibiotics (usually gentamicin or tobramycin) is placed directly in the abscess. In the *Textbook of Rabbit Medicine,* Frances Harcourt-Brown discusses using honey as a topical treatment for abscess cavities. Abscesses often recur in rabbits, especially if the bone is involved, and are a frequent cause of death in pet rabbits.

In a situation where immediate veterinary care is not available, the owner should cut away the fur, bathe the abscess in hot water, and wash it with an antiseptic such as betadine or iodine. Then gently squeeze the pus out and bathe it again with betadine. Coat with unpasteurized honey. Repeat daily until the inflammation recedes and the abscess heals. Follow up this home care with veterinary care as soon as possible.

PREVENTION: Abscesses in rabbits often occur where the rabbit was bitten or received another wound. Always wash wounds with antibacterial solution to help prevent the formation of an abscess. A good diet with adequate fiber and calcium may help prevent abscesses.

Abscesses, teeth

CAUSAL AGENT: *Fusobacterium nucleatum, Prevotella* spp., *Peptostreptococcus micros,* various other bacteria including (rarely) *Pasteurella* spp.

SYMPTOMS: Tearing if abscess is in upper jaw, anorexia, drooling, and/or failure to groom.

TREATMENT: In the past veterinarians often treated dental abscesses on the assumption the primary bacteria present were *Pasteurella* species. Recently, researchers have found other bacteria to be more common in these abscesses, bacteria that do not respond to antibiotics normally used in treating *Pasteurella*. As with other abscesses, complete excision is the best treatment, but this is difficult with dental abscesses. The affected teeth should be removed, the abscess drained and treated with antibiotic beads. Affected rabbits will most likely need to be syringe fed during recovery.

PREVENTION: Abscesses are common in rabbits with tooth infections. They can occur when teeth are fractured (from trimming or a fall where the rabbit strikes his head), and also from wounds sustained in the mouth area. A proper diet and care when handling a rabbit or trimming its teeth are preventative measures that can be taken.

Clostridiosis *(Enterotoxemia)*

CAUSAL AGENT: Toxin produced by *Clostridium difficile, Cl. spiroforme, Cl. perfringens.*

SYMPTOMS: Watery diarrhea or no feces, enlarged abdomen, lethargy, rough coat.

TREATMENT: Cholestyramine (also used as a preventative), metronidazole (Flagyl®).

TRANSMISSION: This organism is thought to be normally present in the gastrointestinal tract of the rabbit, but stress and treatment with penicillin can cause the population of the bacteria to rise to dangerous numbers (between 40–80 percent of rabbits develop clostridiosis after receiving oral penicillin). Clostridiosis is most common in young rabbits four to eight weeks old, but can occur in any age of rabbit.

PREVENTION: Reduce stress, feed young rabbits a low-carbohydrate, high-fiber diet.

Colibacillosis

CAUSAL AGENT: *Escherichia coli.*

SYMPTOMS: In very young rabbits, a severe yellowish diarrhea followed by death. In older rabbits, diarrhea. This usually only affects very young, unweaned rabbits.

Treatment: Antibiotics in mild cases.

TRANSMISSION: Some authors have suggested that a rabbit could potentially contract this disease by stepping in infective dog or cat feces and then cleaning it off his feet. This would be extremely unlikely, but perhaps possible with a stressed or ill rabbit.

PREVENTION: Good sanitation. *E. coli* is not normally in the rabbit GI tract, but could possibly gain a foothold if the rabbit is stressed or ill.

Pasteurellosis

CAUSAL AGENT: *Pasteurella multocida.*

SYMPTOMS: Rabbits with any infection caused by *P. multocida* are considered to have pasteurellosis. There are several different strains of *P. multocida* which vary in pathogenicity. Clinical manifestations of pasteurellosis include but are not limited to snuffles, pneumonia, abscesses, weepy eye, wry neck (head tilt) from ear infections, and genital infections. Infections occurring internally may be difficult to diagnose. Toxins produced by the bacteria may also affect the rabbit.

TREATMENT: Antibiotics (enrofloxacin, penicillin—used with great caution and constant monitoring, chloramphenicol, tetracyclines, gentamicin, trimethoprin-sulfur).

TRANSMISSION: Aerosol, fomites (objects such as cages, dishes, clothing) and direct contact. Acute infections of pasteurellosis are highly contagious, chronic infections are less contagious. Rabbits that have runny noses and are sneezing are most likely to spread the bacteria.

PREVENTION: No effective vaccine has yet been made available, although there have been some promising developments in this direction. A high percentage of rabbits carry the bacteria, but it does not normally get out of control. Stress, a poor diet, dust, and high ammonia levels may make a rabbit more susceptible. The best prevention is to reduce stress and practice good sanitation. Some rabbits appear to have immunity to pasteurellosis, but the factors contributing to this immunity are not yet known.

Pneumonia

CAUSAL AGENT: Usually *Pasteurella multocida,* also *Klebsiella pneumoniae, Staphylococcus aureus.*

SYMPTOMS: Fever, anorexia, lethargy. Pneumonia often develops in rabbits with snuffles.

TREATMENT: Antibiotics (chloramphenicol, oxytetracycline, chlortetracycline, penicillin).

TRANSMISSION: Aerosol, fomites (objects such as cages, dishes, clothing), direct contact.

PREVENTION: Good sanitation and ventilation.

Salmonellosis

CAUSAL AGENT: *Salmonella enteritidis, S. typhimurium.*

SYMPTOMS: Most often no symptoms and sudden death; sometimes anorexia, depression, fever; occasionally diarrhea. Young rabbits are most susceptible.

TREATMENT: Usually not treated. Mortality is high. Rabbits that survive may remain carriers and for that reason are sometimes euthanized.

TRANSMISSION: Ingestion of feed contaminated with poultry or rodent feces or by direct contact. Reptiles and humans also carry this bacteria.

PREVENTION: Reduction of stress, good sanitation. Destroy any feed or bedding contaminated by birds or rodents.

Snuffles *(rhinitis, nasal catarrh)*

CAUSAL AGENT: Usually *Pasteurella multocida,* also *Pseudomonas* sp., *Staphylococcus aureus, Streptococcus* sp., and *Bordetella bronchiseptica.*

SYMPTOMS: Sticky yellowish discharge from nose, ocular discharge, mouth breathing, swelling, bright red mucous membranes in nose, snuffling, sneezing, coughing, lethargy, depression, wry neck (head tilt). Rabbit may have matter caked on front legs from trying to clear the discharge from the nose and eyes. Infection can involve the bones and structures of the head. Snuffles is often a precursor of pneumonia.

TREATMENT: Antibiotics. It is critical to get early veterinary treatment for your rabbit if it displays any of the above symptoms in order to give the rabbit the best chance of survival. Despite the benign-sounding name, snuffles is responsible for many deaths of pet rabbits.

TRANSMISSION: Aerosol, contact, venereal.

PREVENTION: Good sanitation and ventilation, proper diet. Never ignore symptoms of snuffles, and isolate the rabbit from others until his condition is diagnosed by a veterinarian.

Treponematosis *(vent disease, rabbit syphilis, venereal spirochetosis)*

CAUSAL AGENT: *Treponemia papaluiscuniculi.*

SYMPTOMS: Ulcers and scabs on the genitalia. Rabbits may also develop ulcers on the lips, eyelids, ears, face, and paws from grooming themselves. When they do occur on the face and eyelids they may sometimes be mistaken for early signs of myxomatosis.

TREATMENT: Solu-salvarsan inserted under the skin, benzathine penicillin. This bacterium is extremely sensitive to penicillin, and this is one disease where it will probably be necessary to use it. The penicillin should be injected intramuscularly every seven to 10 days.

TRANSMISSION: Usually doe to kit or venereal contact. Rabbit syphilis is not transmissible to humans. Some rabbits may become asymptomatic carriers—rabbits that were infected but show no symptoms until later in life when they become stressed. These rabbits can potentially infect other rabbits.

Tularemia

CAUSAL AGENT: *Francisella tularensis.*

SYMPTOMS: Abscess at initial site, fever, anorexia, depression, rough coat, death. This disease is rare in pet rabbits.

TREATMENT: Antibiotics.

TRANSMISSION: Direct contact, ingestion, aerosol, biting arthropods (especially ticks, mosquitoes, and biting flies). Rodents, cats, and humans can also contract tularemia.

PREVENTION: Control of above arthropods.

Tyzzer's Disease

CAUSAL AGENT: *Clostridium piliformis* (formerly *Bacillus piliformis*).

SYMPTOMS: Watery diarrhea, anorexia, dehydration, lethargy, depression. This disease usually kills rabbits under 12 weeks old within one to three days. In older rabbits the disease is chronic.

TREATMENT: Currently no effective treatment. Oxytetracycline may help somewhat.

TRANSMISSION: Ingestion of contaminated fecal matter from rabbits and possibly rodents and cats.

PREVENTION: Good sanitation and reduction of stress.

viral diseases

There are relatively few viral diseases which may affect your pet rabbit, but two of them (RHD and myxomatosis) are perhaps the most horrific diseases a pet rabbit could contract. For this reason it is a good idea to be familiar with the names and symptoms of those diseases.

Myxomatosis

CAUSAL AGENT: *Myxoma virus* (*Leporipoxvirus* sp.).

SYMPTOMS: Milky, pus-like discharge from eyes, nasal discharge, lethargy, fever, labored breathing, anorexia, rough coat, swelling of genitals, lips, nose, eyelids, and base of ears. There are several strains of myxomatosis, some more virulent than others. In some of the less virulent strains, skin tumors occur in large numbers and then may regress. The strain endemic to the western coast of the U.S. in California and Oregon is rapidly lethal with lesser development of symptoms. The severity of this disease is greater at low environmental temperatures and lower at high environmental temperatures.

TREATMENT: There is no effective treatment for this disease. Very few affected rabbits survive, although some have recovered given intense nursing care including warmth, fluid therapy, nutritional support, and antibiotics. Rabbits that do survive develop partial to total immunity. In the U.S. the disease is restricted to the coastal area of California and Oregon, where there are outbreaks in the summer months about every eight to 10 years.

TRANSMISSION: Direct contact, biting arthropods (especially fleas, mosquitoes, fur mites, and biting flies). Fleas are of special concern because of their relatively long lives and the potential for other pets to bring them into a home.

PREVENTION: A vaccine is available in Europe. In the U.S. the best prevention is to control of above arthropods. Be sure to treat pets for fleas if you live in an area with myxomatosis.

Oral Papillomatosis

CAUSAL AGENT: *Papillomavirus* sp. (distinct from Shope papilloma virus).

SYMPTOMS: Warts on bottom of tongue and floor of mouth.

TREATMENT: None necessary—the warts usually regress in a few weeks, and the rabbits remain healthy.

TRANSMISSION: Contact.

PREVENTION: This is common in cottontails. It is most often found in domestic rabbits in the northeastern part of the U.S.

Papillomatosis

CAUSAL AGENT: *Papillomavirus* sp. (Shope papilloma virus). Symptoms: Large horn-like warts on the neck, shoulders, ears, abdomen.

TREATMENT: These warts usually regress in a few months. Most rabbits remain healthy, but some will develop squamous cell carcinoma (see "cancer" in this chapter).

TRANSMISSION: Arthropods that transmit disease, especially mosquitoes and rabbit ticks.

PREVENTION: This is a common disease of cottontails and jackrabbits. If you live in areas with wild rabbits, control of above arthropods is critical for prevention.

RHD *(rabbit hemorrhagic disease, RCD, rabbit calicivirus disease, RCV, rabbit calicivirus, necrotic hepatitis, rabbit plague, rabbit viral septicemia, viral hemorrhagic pneumonia, VHD, viral hemorrhagic disease).*

CAUSAL AGENT: *Lagovirus* sp. (a calicivirus).

SYMPTOMS: Most often death with no previous symptoms. When symptoms do appear, death will usually follow within six to 24 hours. Symptoms include fever, anorexia, lethargy, rapid breathing, bleeding from the nose, rectum, and mouth, foamy nasal discharge, convulsions. Mortality nears 100 percent, usually within 48 hours of initial exposure, although rarely a rabbit may survive. Very young rabbits (usually five weeks old or less) frequently do not develop symptoms or die, but may become carriers of the virus.

TREATMENT: There is no effective treatment for this disease.

TRANSMISSION: This virus may be transmitted through the air, urine, feces, saliva, and on objects. This disease is *highly* contagious, and will rapidly infect all the rabbits at a premise. The virus often survives past 30 days, and occasionally up to 105 days. At lower temperatures it can survive up to 225 days.

PREVENTION: A killed virus vaccine is available in Europe, Asia, and Australia, but it is not available in the U.S. at this time. Currently there is no vaccine available in the U.S., although researchers are currently working on different possibilities.

The best prevention for U.S. residents at this time is cleanliness and caution. Always wash hands when coming indoors. If you live in an area near an outbreak, change clothes and bathe before handling your rabbits. Do not wear street shoes inside your home. Check the Internet often for information on this disease and any new U.S. outbreaks.

HISTORY: RHD was first reported in China in 1984. From there it spread to the rest of Asia, Europe, and Africa. In 1988 it was reported in Mexico (although later declared eradicated there), and has also been reported in Cuba, South America, New Zealand, and Australia. It was not reported in the U.S. until 1994. The next confirmed outbreak in the U.S. occurred in Crawford County, Iowa, in 1999. In 2001 another outbreak originated in Utah county, Utah, and in December of the same year rabbits in New York tested positive for RHD.

Rabbit Pox

CAUSAL AGENT: *Orthopoxvirus* sp.

SYMPTOMS: Discharge from eyes and nose, fever, skin rash, swelling of face and genitals. Rabbit may die within a week to several weeks.

TREATMENT: There is no treatment.

TRANSMISSION: Contact. The disease is not transmissible to man.

PREVENTION: This disease is mostly found in laboratory rabbits.

gastrointestinal conditions

It is a rare rabbit owner who will escape having to deal with some kind of gastrointestinal condition in their rabbit at one time or another. Rabbits' digestive systems are susceptible to being upset. Although most of the gastrointestinal problems a rabbit may have are relatively easy to treat if caught in time, time is the critical factor. Therefore it is important that rabbit owners be able to recognize the early symptoms of gastrointestinal problems.

Acute Bloat *(tympany)*

CAUSE: Gas may accumulate due to hairball or other obstruction, ileus, infection, change in diet, twisted intestine.

SYMPTOMS: Enlarged abdomen, anorexia, depression, failure to defecate, subnormal temperature, loud gurgling from the rabbit's stomach, signs of severe pain such as grinding teeth, sitting in a hunched-up posture. This condition has a rapid onset and the rabbit may die within 24 hours if not treated.

TREATMENT: Administration of an analgesic, ringer's solution, and application of external heat. A stomach tube can be inserted for decompression (the stomach should never be decompressed by needle puncture), followed by administration of simethicone. Depending on the cause of the bloat, surgery may be the only chance to save the rabbit. However, the vet will have a difficult time telling which cases require surgery, and the rabbit's chance of surviving such surgery is low.

PREVENTION: A high-fiber diet. Diets which are too high in protein can contribute to this condition. Give rabbit good quality fresh vegetables in quantities not exceeding one cup per day for a five- to six-pound rabbit. Avoid cabbage and related vegetables.

Hairballs *(trichobezoars, wool block)* and gastrointestinal obstructions

CAUSE: Of hairballs, mass of hair in stomach which blocks pylorus. Other causes of gastrointestinal obstruction include tumors, carpet fibers, items such as dried peas and beans.

SYMPTOMS: Polydipsia, anorexia, few feces or no feces, weight loss, enlarged abdomen, lethargy. Death usually will occur two to three weeks after fecal pellets stop if untreated.

(Note: Hair in the feces is not necessarily a sign of a trichobezoar. Some hair in the intestinal tract is normal in rabbits. If a rabbit eats enough hay, the hair is passed safely through without the formation of a blocking mass.)

TREATMENT: Many veterinarians now consider the most common cause of hairballs to be a lack of intestinal motility from stress or other medical conditions. Increasing dietary fiber (lots of grass hay and some fresh vegetables) and fluids may be enough to solve the problem, and in more severe cases motility drugs such as Propulsid® (cisapride) or Reglan® (metoclopramide) can be prescribed. More traditional treatments include giving 10 ml/day of fresh or frozen pineapple juice and an inch of Laxatone® or Petromalt®. (The latter is recommended only if the rabbit is not dehydrated—some vets feel that if these preparations are given to a dehydrated rabbit it may prevent the hairball from dissolving.) As a last resort, a vet may attempt to remove the mass surgically. Most hairballs removed surgically are found to be small, rock-hard hairballs lodged in the pylorus. However, rabbits have a poor survival rate from this kind of surgery.

Rarely, an object such as a dried pea which is causing an intestinal blockage will move through the intestine on its own, causing recurring symptoms until it has passed. More often, blockages from objects such as dried legumes and carpet fibers are likely to result in acute bloat, and early diagnosis and surgery are probably the only chance to save the rabbit.

PREVENTION: This is a condition where prevention is critical. Groom rabbits regularly. Rabbits should always have access to sufficient dietary roughage in the form of good timothy hay. If a rabbit is pulling out and consuming excessive hair, try to find the cause. Check the teeth to be sure they are not maloccluded. A rabbit may also pull his hair out because of stress or boredom. Be sure he or she has adequate toys and that the cage is not located in a stressful area.

Rabbits with dental problems may be more likely

to swallow food whole, and should be watched carefully. Do not feed any rabbit items like dried peas, corn,
and beans. If your rabbit is digging carpet and consuming fibers, keep him out of the area or block him from
digging (see "Rabbit Proofing," Chapter 3).

Ileus *(chronic stasis), gastrointestinal hypomotility, G.I. stasis*

CAUSE: Ileus is a slowdown or shutdown of the normal
movement of the intestines. It can be caused by bad
diet, stress, pain, intestinal blockage, and many diseases
and conditions. When this normal intestinal movement
slows, harmful bacteria grow in the rabbit's cecum.
Toxins from the bacteria accumulate and may poison
the rabbit. Gas may also accumulate. Eventually the
liver is damaged. This is a very serious condition which
can kill your rabbit.

SYMPTOMS: Enlarged abdomen, anorexia, fewer fecal pellets or smaller fecal pellets, low body temperature,
lethargy.

TREATMENT: Treatment strategy is to hydrate the rabbit and
get the intestine moving again. Increase fiber in the rabbit's diet, give simethicone for gas, and an analgesic if the
rabbit shows signs of pain. A motility drug such as Reglan®
(metoclopramide) or Propulsid® (cisapride) can be administered. The former drug stimulates the upper intestinal
tract, and the latter helps restore normal contractions to
the lower tract. Although it does not naturally occur in
rabbits, there is some evidence that acidophilus will help
rabbits with ileus because of its inhibitory effect on
Escherichia coli and other harmful bacteria. The most helpful probiotic is a cecotroph from a healthy rabbit.

PREVENTION: Diet and exercise. The rabbit should have a good high-fiber diet. Diets too high in protein can contribute to the problem.

Mucoid Enteropathy

CAUSE: In question. No consistent association with a pathogenic organism has been found. It may be related to ileus or an imbalance in the flora of the intestines.

SYMPTOMS: Anorexia, enlarged abdomen, low temperature, dehydration, polydipsia, severe pain, depression, mucinous diarrhea. This is most common in rabbits seven to 14 weeks old.

TREATMENT: Electrolytes, antibiotics.

TRANSMISSION: Unknown.

PREVENTION: Stress reduction.

Volvulus

CAUSE: Intestine twists upon itself, causing a blockage. Severe gas may contribute to this condition, as may a lack of muscle tone.

SYMPTOMS: This condition has a rapid onset. Rabbit may have appeared completely healthy just a few hours earlier. Symptoms include enlarged abdomen, anorexia, constipation, dehydration, rapid heart beat, acute pain, rapid deterioration due to endotoxemia.

TREATMENT: Rabbits with this condition will die in less than 24 hours from onset of symptoms if not treated. Surgical correction of the intestine is the only treatment, but the rabbit rarely survives such surgery.

PREVENTION: Feed rabbit high-fiber diet. Restrict fresh vegetables to a cup per day for a five-pound rabbit and avoid cabbage and similar vegetables. Be sure rabbit gets adequate exercise. This condition may be more common in older rabbits. If your rabbit exhibits symptoms of bloat, treat with simethicone immediately. Immediate treatment of bloat can prevent complications such as volvulus from developing, and simethicone will not harm the rabbit even if it turns out the rabbit is not bloated.

other diseases and conditions

In this section I have included broken bones, dental problems, heat prostration, cancer, and other conditions which did not fit easily into any of the other categories.

Allergies and environmental irritants

CAUSE: Irritation by allergens or environmental irritants such as cigarette smoke, dust, high ammonia concentrations, fumes from household chemicals and preparations.

SYMPTOMS: Sneezing, coughing, ocular and nasal discharge. Irritation of the respiratory membranes by allergens and irritants makes rabbits more susceptible to bacterial pathogens such as *Pasteurella multocida.*

TREATMENT: Possible bacterial causes must first be eliminated. Identification of allergen and its elimination from environment if possible. Some rabbits have allergies to particular grains which can be eliminated from their diets. If the allergen cannot be identified and the reaction of the rabbit is severe, allergy can be treated with antihistamines or corticosteroids.

PREVENTION: Good sanitation and good ventilation. Do not use strong household chemicals near rabbits (or products with strong fumes such as stain and varnish).

Broken Back *(vertebral fracture or dislocation)*

CAUSE: Usually fracture or dislocation of the seventh lumbar vertebra (backbone) from improper handling, stepping on a rabbit, shutting it in a door, or self-injury when the rabbit is startled or frightened. Older rabbits and rabbits that don't receive enough exercise are more prone to this injury because of reduced bone density, as are rabbits with inadequate calcium in their diets.

SYMPTOMS: Rabbit remains in corner of cage, is lethargic, displays urinary and fecal incontinence, and paralysis of hindquarters.

TREATMENT: If the spinal cord is not completely severed or seriously damaged, this condition sometimes resolves itself in three to five days as the swelling around the spinal cord recedes. Corticosteroid treatment with cage rest and nursing is sometimes prescribed. Rabbits with moderate damage that do not remain incontinent will often heal within six to eight weeks of cage rest with intensive nursing. If the paralysis continues after a week or the rabbit remains incontinent the outlook is not good. However, the number of owners who continue to care for rabbits with this condition instead of euthanizing their pets is increasing, and special supplies are available to improve the quality of the rabbit's life (see Chapter 9).

PREVENTION: Correct handling of rabbits is the best way to prevent this injury. Always support the hindquarters and hold the rabbit *firmly* (see Chapter 4). A rabbit which kicks and twists while being held can easily fracture its spine. Do not let very young children handle a rabbit. If your rabbit begins to jump from your arms while you are standing, drop to your knees so the rabbit has a shorter distance to fall. Do your best to keep your rabbits from being seriously frightened, as a very fright-ened rabbit is likely to panic and throw itself against the cage or room walls, risking fractures. Be sure your rabbit is out of his cage often enough to get adequate exercise so he does not become more prone to the injury through loss of bone density. Diets deficient in calcium may also predispose your rabbit to spinal fracture.

Cancer

SYMPTOMS: Symptoms of uterine, mammary, and testicular cancer are tumors, usually multiple. With uterine adeno-carcinoma there may be a vaginal discharge, often bloody. This may appear as a red patch in the center of a puddle of urine. Symptoms of lymphoma (lymphocarcinoma) are abdominal masses, anemia, and lymph node enlarge-ment. Lymphoma is most common in rabbits between eight months to 1½ years, and neoplasms are most often found on liver, spleen, and kidneys. Eyes are also a com-mon site for lymphomas, and may be seen as a dark lump or spot on the eye. Squamous cell cancers may develop from horny warts and can metastasize to any organ.

TREATMENT: Uterine cancer is difficult to treat, as it usual-ly metastasizes, frequently to the lungs. It is slow devel-oping, but fatal. Mammary cancer also usually metasta-sizes. Corticosteroids may slow the growth of lym-phoma, although in general the prognosis for rabbits with lymphoma is poor. In cases where the lymphoma has developed in a limb, amputation of the limb may be advised. When lymphoma develops in eye tissue, the rabbit can sometimes be treated successfully by having the eye removed. Squamous cell carcinomas need early treatment and removal.

PREVENTION: The best way to prevent the most common cancer of rabbits, uterine cancer, is to have does spayed before they are two years old. (Dutch, Californian, and New Zealand rabbits have the highest incidences of uterine cancer.) Mammary and testicular cancers are also less common in altered rabbits. Certain rabbits may carry a gene that makes them more susceptible to lymphoma, but the owner will not be able to tell by breed.

Heat Exhaustion *(heat prostration, heat stress, heat stroke)*

CAUSE: Prolonged exposure to temperatures above 85 degrees F (28 degrees C), especially with humidity over 70 percent.

SYMPTOMS: Weakness; lethargy; rapid or labored breathing; polydipsia; anorexia, drooling; rectal temperature above 104 degrees F (40 degrees C); blue-tinged mouth, nose, ears; incoordination; convulsions; coma; death.

TREATMENT: Spray the rabbit with a mist of water, wrap rabbit in a cool dampened cloth, immerse rabbit in cool (not cold) water, control seizures.

PREVENTION: Heat exhaustion is more common in rabbits with thick coats, obese rabbits, and older rabbits. On hot days freeze a plastic bottle or carton of water and put it in the cage with the rabbit, place a refrigerated ceramic tile in the cage, put ice cubes in the rabbit's water dish, or have a fan blowing the air near (but not directly on) the rabbits. Do not locate a rabbit cage in direct sunlight or next to a heat vent.

Hutch Burn *(urine burn)*

CAUSE: Membranes of the genitals and anus become

inflamed and chapped from contact with urine. Secondary infections may occur.

SYMPTOMS: Swelling of anus and genital region, brownish crusts over genital area, oozing pus.

TREATMENT: Trim matted fur and apply antibiotic ointment. Clean rabbit's cage.

PREVENTION: Hutch burn is most commonly seen when a rabbit hutch or cage has dirt floors that are wet with urine. Keep the surfaces of your rabbit's cage clean and dry at all times. Incontinent rabbits or rabbits that dribble or urinate excessively from other conditions may develop hutch burn.

Inflammation of the ear *(ear infection, otitis externa, otitis media, otitis interna)*

CAUSE: When the external ear canal is affected, often ear mites. Sometimes secondary infections resulting from a heavy infestation of ear mites can damage the inner ear. *Pasteurella multocida* is often present in middle and inner ear infections.

SYMPTOMS: When the external ear canal is affected: head shaking, pawing at the ears, scratching. When it affects the middle ear there are often no symptoms. In one study, about one third of adult rabbits were found to have otitis media, or inflammation of the middle ear. There may be some hearing loss, but hearing loss in a rabbit is often hard for an owner to recognize. When the inner ear is affected, head tilt is a common symptom.

TREATMENT: If the cause is ear mites, treatment with ivermectin followed by antibiotic therapy if a secondary infection has developed. *P. multocida* infections of the ear should be treated as for pasteurellosis.

Lead Poisoning, heavy metal poisoning

CAUSE: Ingestion of lead, usually through chewing of surfaces painted with lead-based paint, or ingestion of other objects containing lead of other heavy metals such as zinc.

SYMPTOMS: Lethargy, depression, anorexia, weight loss. Lead poisoning may depress the immune system and make the rabbit susceptible to diseases such as pneumonia.

TREATMENT: For lead, subcutaneous administration of Ca-EDTA. If ileus is present, treat with cisapride or metaclopramide.

PREVENTION: If you allow your rabbit to roam free in your house, watch to be sure it does not chew on anything painted with older lead-based paint.

Malocclusion *(mandibular prognathism, brachygnathism)*

CAUSE: Normal wearing of teeth does not occur. This happens most often with the upper and lower incisors, rarely the molars. In young rabbits it is usually an inherited condition (autosomal recessive with incomplete penetrance), although it can sometimes be caused by a rabbit pulling on cage wires with his teeth. If it occurs later in life it may be a result of a trauma, tumor, or infection. It can also be caused by tooth trimming in older rabbits.

The inherited condition is more common in dwarf rabbits. These rabbits were bred for a cuteness of face resulting from a skull shaped more like that of a juvenile, and the teeth may not meet correctly in this type of skull.

SYMPTOMS: Dermatitis on chin, drooling, weight loss, anorexia, fur pulling, pawing at the mouth, piercing of mouth by teeth, ulcerations of the lips and tongue, abscesses in the mouth, eventual death from starvation if not treated.

TREATMENT: Clean around the teeth if hair and other debris accumulate. Clip or file teeth frequently (they grow about 2 mm/week). Have your veterinarian show you how to do this, or if you are not comfortable doing it, take the rabbit in regularly to have it done. Improperly clipping teeth can lead to fracture and infection. In severe cases of malocclusion affected teeth may be surgically removed. Some veterinarians do not recommend extraction because it is extremely difficult to remove all the root tissue. If any remains new teeth can develop, sometimes growing out of the cheek or into the eye, requiring euthanasia of the animal.

PREVENTION: Acquired malocclusion may sometimes be prevented by adequate calcium in the diet and by providing the rabbit with grass and safe sticks to chew. If tooth trimming is necessary for an older rabbit it should be done carefully, as excessive trauma when trimming teeth can cause malocclusion.

Sore Hocks (ulcerative pododermatitis)

CAUSE: Trauma to skin on bottom of feet with development of secondary infections (usually *Staphyloccus aureus*) that may extend to the bone.

SYMPTOMS: Anorexia, loss of weight, crusty ulcers on hind feet. Rabbit may sit with his weight on his front feet and tiptoe when walking. Death can occur in rare cases.

TREATMENT: Bathe sores with warm water, treat with topical antibiotic ointment such as mupirocin. Some rabbits will tolerate light bandages on the feet, others will not. Recurrence is common.

PREVENTION: This condition is more frequently seen in the large breeds of rabbits, rex rabbits, older rabbits, incontinent rabbits, rabbits not given enough exercise, and rabbits living in cages with wire floors. Watch for bald places on the bottoms of the hind feet. Rabbits don't have pads on their feet like cats and dogs, and need hair to cushion their feet. If your rabbit cage has wire floors, provide the rabbit with a piece of plywood to sit on. Size of cage may also be a factor; be sure your rabbit has room to move around. If your rabbit suffers from incontinence, be sure you keep both the rabbit and his cage clean.

Splayleg

CAUSE: This is usually a genetic condition although it can have other causes. It most often affects the hind limbs, although the forelimbs can also be affected. Genetic splayleg affecting the hind limbs is caused by a mutant autosomal gene inherited in a simple autosomal recessive pattern. It is seen most often in lops.

SYMPTOMS: Hind legs are splayed. There may be skeletal deformity. Growth may be slightly stunted. The legs may remain functional or become partially or totally paralyzed.

TREATMENT: Rabbits with splayleg are usually alert and responsive. With care they may live several months to years.

Urolithiasis *(stones in the urinary tract—kidneys, ureter, bladder, or urethra)*

CAUSE: Precipitation of salt crystals (calcium carbonate and tricyclic phosphate) out of urine when the pH of the urine reaches 8.5–9.5 (normal urine pH is 8.2). When the crystals come together, they can form uroliths, or "stones." Factors thought to lead to stone formation include too much calcium in the rabbit's diet, not enough water, and infections.

SYMPTOMS: Thick creamy urine, sludgy urine, failure to use litter box for urine, inability to urinate, straining to urinate with hind leg and tail tremors, anorexia, weight loss, depression, symptoms of pain. If the rabbit becomes unable to urinate, immediate veterinary treatment is necessary to save the rabbit's life.

TREATMENT: Fluids, manual expression of bladder, reduction of dietary calcium, treatment to acidify urine. Other treatments include flushing the bladder and surgical removal of bladder stones (uroliths).

PREVENTION: This condition is more common in males. Frequent urination may help prevent urolith formation, so be sure your rabbits have fresh water available at all times. Limit treats like crackers and bread which are high in calcium. Although the connection is not proven, it has long been assumed that excessive dietary calcium is a cause of uroliths. To reduce calcium in your rabbit's diet, cut the amount of alfalfa-based pellets given your rabbit and supplement the diet with rolled oats, timothy-based pellets, and green vegetables. Remember, some calcium is necessary in a rabbit's diet for healthy teeth and good bones.

Wet Dewlap (slobbers, moist dermatitis)

CAUSE: Fold of skin on doe's neck stays wet from drinking water or drooling. It may then become inflamed and develop a bacterial infection. A similar condition can develop in bucks.

Symptoms: Dewlap is visibly moist and swollen. Hair loss may occur. In cases where it becomes infected with *Pseudomonas* the dewlap may appear greenish.

Treatment: Clip fur from dewlap, treat with topical or systemic antibiotics. Treat any underlying dental problems that may be causing drooling.

Prevention: Provide does with water bottles instead of water crocks to drink from. If the condition was caused by drooling because of maloccluded teeth, keep the teeth trimmed.

Weepy eye, conjunctivitis

Cause: Irritated eye from dust, dirt, pollen, bacterial infection, blocked tear ducts.

Symptoms: Ocular discharge (epiphora). Tears may run down cheeks when the rabbit shuts its eye. Discharge will sometimes crust on the eye (in this case the cause is usually bacterial).

Treatment: Opthalmic ointments. If the cause is bacterial it will most often (40–60 percent) be *Staphylococcus aureus*. *Pasteurella multocida* accounts for about 12 percent. Penicillin, streptomycin, and topically administered chlortetracycline are used to treat bacterial infections. Minor eye irritation can be treated with Gentocin®, eye ointment or drops.

Transmission: If bacterial, by direct contact and through contact with fomites (objects).

Prevention: Weepy eye from blocked tear ducts is more common in lops. Keep cages and litter boxes clean to prevent ammonia build-up from causing tearing.

a final thought

to anyone who has persevered reading this book to this page, it may indeed seem that rabbits are fragile creatures, difficult to care for and to keep healthy. In truth, it is only that they and their needs are unfamiliar to us. After a little time has passed, it becomes second nature to monitor a rabbit's health and diet and keep its area clean and safe. My house rabbits take very little more time to care for than my two house cats, and with the exception of my special needs rabbit, my rabbits have been just as healthy and hardy as my cats.

Rabbits force us to learn new ways of looking at things and new ways of doing things. Rabbits, being the cautious prey animals they are, will not be hurried into relationships. They make us slow down and take time to know and appreciate them and earn their trust. They require us to become more perceptive, to learn to read the meaning behind the

A rabbit companion can bring joy and contentment.

slight turning of an ear or the nudge of a head. They teach us to live in the moment, to find joy in simply being alive. Perhaps, in this fast-paced, hectic, ever more violent world, that is their greatest gift.

resources for rabbit owners

there are many shelters. organizations devoted to the welfare of domestic rabbits, and rabbit supply businesses in existence today. I cannot list them all, so I have decided to limit my listings primarily to those with which I am familiar.

rabbit health resources

House Rabbit Resource Network

P.O. Box 152432
Austin, TX 78715
www.rabbitresource.net
The House Rabbit Resource Network works to educate people about keeping rabbits in their homes and locates foster homes for rescued rabbits. They also sell an inexpensive ($17.95 at the time of this writing) emergency kit for rabbit owners. I highly recommend the HRRN kit as a good basic kit.

K-9 Carts

656 SE Bayshore Dr., Ste. #2
Oak Harbor, WA 98277
www.k9carts.com
This company is one of my exceptions to including only those companies I have dealt with because I have not yet needed a cart for a rabbit. K-9 Carts makes carts for disabled pets (including rabbits) which are custom built according to the animal's weight, measurements, and needs. I was informed by K-9 Carts

that they have been building carts for rabbits for over 20 years, and that most of the rabbits (about 95 percent) have adapted quite well to using a cart. Carts are not as expensive as you might expect—a cart for a rabbit would cost from $250 up.

RHD (VHD) in the U.S. Coalition
www.kindplanet.org/vhd/vhd.html
Unfortunately, this Web page is no longer active, but it is kept up so that concerned individuals can still read the information about RHD. I urge every rabbit owner to read the information still available on this inactive site. It may save your rabbit's life.

shelters and sanctuaries

Adopt-a-Rabbit Program, The Fund for Animal's Rabbit Sanctuary
P.O. Box 80036
Simpsonville, SC 29680
www.adopt-a-rabbit.org
This South Carolina sanctuary provides a permanent home for about 100 rabbits which have come from shelters, breeders, laboratories, and unfit homes. It is unusual in that actual physical adoptions do not take place since the rescued rabbits are guaranteed a home for life in the "rabbitats" at the sanctuary. Adoptions are "virtual," that is, your donation helps provide care for the rabbits, and you are sent a picture and history of "your" rabbit for a donation of $20 or more. People residing near Simpsonville, SC may inquire about volunteer work at the sanctuary.

Best Friends Animal Sanctuary
5001 Angel Canyon Rd.
Kanab, UT 84741-5001
www.bestfriends.org

This large, no-kill sanctuary includes a Bunny House with many wonderful rabbits waiting to be adopted. Check out the Web site to learn about the rabbits currently available for adoption.

Best Friends also sponsors Best Friends Network, a network of animal lovers and organizations across the country dedicated to no more homeless pets. People who call or e-mail requesting information are put in contact with a volunteer in their area. Visit the Best Friends Web site for more information on Best Friends Network.

Brambley Hedge Rabbit Rescue

P.O. Box 54506
Phoenix, AZ 85078-4506
www.bhrabbit.rescue.org
Brambley Hedge is one of my exceptions to including only those organizations I have dealt with because I have heard such wonderful things about them from people I trust. Brambley Hedge volunteers rescue abused and unwanted domestic rabbits and run a non-profit, no-kill shelter. They have placed many of their rabbits in good homes over the fifteen years the have been in operation. Volunteers at Brambley Hedge are also active in educating the public on proper rabbit care.

BunnyLuv Rabbit Resource Center

16742 Stagg Street #104
Van Nuys, CA 91406
www.bunnyluv.org
To quote from the Web page, "BLRRC is a non-profit, no-kill animal welfare organization, offering education, adoption, and care, plus services and supplies for domestic rabbits and the humans who luv them." See also entry for BunnyLuv Essentials under Rabbit Supplies.

Double "D" Ranch
Deb & Dale Olon-Wes
1046 Polk Street
Erie, PA 16503-1548.
www.Double-D-Ranch.net
The Double "D" Ranch is a fairly new rabbit rescue/shelter. About three years ago, Deb began learning how to give her own rabbits better care and living conditions. Soon she and Dale became known as "rabbit people," and they were being offered abandoned rabbits. The Double "D" Ranch came into being. Located in their home, the Double "D" currently has about 30 rabbits. For a young shelter they are doing wonderful work—Dale tells me they have placed 52 rabbits in homes over the past year and a half.

Four Corners Bunnies
Debby Widolf
351 Spruce Mesa Drive
Durango, CO 81301
http://ourworld.compuserve.com/homepages/nanetteb
Debby Widolf is a House Rabbit Society fosterer and educator. Four Corners Bunnies rescues and finds good homes for abused and abandoned rabbits in southwestern Colorado and Albuquerque, New Mexico. Debby also sells handmade "lolly-lops" (stuffed cloth bunnies filled with seed). The proceeds go toward the rescue and care of domestic rabbits in the Four Corners area (where the states of Utah, Colorado, Arizona, and New Mexico meet).

The House Rabbit Society promotes keeping domestic rabbits as spayed/neutered house pets in homes where they will receive proper attention and care. Members are active in educating people in the proper care of domestic rabbits as well as rescuing, fostering, and finding homes for the rabbits. The HRS has many chapters operating throughout the United States. Check the HRS Web site at www.rabbit.org for one in your area.

rabbit supply businesses

Bunny Bytes: Outfitters of the Urban Rabbit
P.O. Box 1581
Kent, WA 98035
www.bunnybytes.com
Bunny Bytes offers a wide variety of products for you and your rabbit, including toys, treats, supplies, and gifts. To quote from the Bunny Bytes website, "Our mission is to improve the health and well-being of house rabbits by offering high quality, environmentally friendly and innovative products."

The Busy Bunny®
P.O. Box 1023
San Bruno, CA 94066-4120
www.busybunny.com
My bunnies just loved their willow tunnel and baskets of goodies from The Busy Bunny. This company sells many safe treats and supplies for your rabbits as well as books, note cards, and other rabbit-related items for rabbit owners. I have always had excellent service from this company.

Bunny Heaven
16 Mt. Bethel Road
PMB 262
Warren, NJ 07059
www.bunnyheaven.com
No supplies for rabbits are offered here, but rather bunny merchandise for the rabbit-loving person: clothes, jewelry, accessories, and household items with rabbit themes. The Web site states that "one of the goals of Bunny Heaven is to promote the welfare of rabbits in general and house rabbits in particular." Orders accepted by Internet, phone, fax, and mail.

BunnyLuv Essentials

16742 Stagg St. #104

Van Nuys, CA 91406

www.bunnyluv.com

Hay, pellets, litter, litter boxes, grooming supplies, toys, dishes, and more are available at BunnyLuv. This is where I ordered the cardboard "castle" my rabbits love so much. See entry for BunnyLuv Rabbit Resource Center under Shelters, Sanctuaries, and Rabbit Welfare Organizations.

KW Cages

9565 Pathway Street, Ste. B

Santee, CA 92071

www.KWcages.com

KW Cages carries several different styles of pet rabbit cages as well as transport cages, exercise pens, and many other useful rabbit supplies and books. A print catalog is available.

Leith Petwerks Inc.

P.O. Box 453

151 East Main St.

Gosport, IN 47433

www.petwerks.com

Leith Petwerks produces wonderfully roomy "bunny abodes" large enough for even the largest house bunnies. They also sell other rabbit supplies, including many safe items for your rabbit to chew. Leith Petwerks has a "Hungry Bunny Reorder Program" through which you can have your rabbits' basic supplies (hay, feed, litter) sent automatically every two weeks to every three months.

Morton Jones Pet Care Products

925 3rd Street

Ramona, CA 92065

www.mortonjones.com

Morton Jones sells many rabbit supplies, including (among other products) galvanized steel cages, transport cages of various sizes, waterers, and litter pans. A print catalog is available.

Future Pets.com
11600 Manchaca Road, #101
Austin, TX 78748
www.petexpo.net
Future Pets carries high-sided small animal cages that work well for smaller rabbits, as well as a larger cage especially for rabbits. Future Pets also carries grooming items for rabbit owners.

plants potentially harmful to rabbits*

Aloe vera
Amaryllis
Anemone
Arum lily
Asparagus fern
Azalea
Begonia
Bleeding heart
Bluebell
Buckthorn
Buttercup
Calendula
Calla lily
Carnation
Castor beans
Chrysanthemums
Clematis
Columbine
Coral Bells
Creeping Charlie
Crocus
Daffodil
Delphinium
Dieffenbachia
Dracaena
Fig
Four o'clock
Foxglove

Holly
Hyacinth
Hydrangea
Impatiens
Inkberry
Iris
Ivy
Jerusalem cherry
Jimson weed
Juniper
Laburnum
Leyland cypress
Lily of the valley
Lobelia
Lupine
Milkweed
Mistletoe
Morning glory
Mountain laurel
Narcissus
Oleander
Parsnip
Peony
Periwinkle
Potato shoots
Primrose
Privet
Pyracantha berry

Rhododendron	Schefflera
Rhubarb leaves	Star-of-Bethlehem
Rhus (sumac)	Sweet pea
Rubber plant	Thuja
Rue	Tulip
St. John's wort	Wisteria

Although you should be careful what plants a house rabbit has access to, don't panic if your rabbit eats a plant on this list. If the rabbit only consumes a little, you will probably notice no ill effects at all. Even if a rabbit eats enough of a plant to cause symptoms of poisoning to become apparent, he will probably be able to be treated successfully. Symptoms of plant poisoning vary, and could include loss of coordination, hypothermia, drooling, gastrointestinal problems, rough coat, and paralysis, depending upon the toxins involved.

---

*Opinions on plants that may harm rabbits vary widely. Frances Harcourt-Brown, author of *Textbook of Rabbit Medicine,* points out that toxicity varies depending on how much of the plant is eaten, how often, whether it is fresh or dried, and what part of the plant is consumed. Often plants that are known to be toxic to other pets, such as cats and dogs, are listed as toxic to rabbits although there may be no actual reports to substantiate the claims.

The concerned rabbit owner is better off being more cautious than less. I have included many plants in this list for which I have no literature citations to back up claims of toxicity to rabbits.

photo contributors

Brambley Hedge Rabbit Rescue, pp. 18, 147, 237.
www.bhrabbitrescue.org

Kim Dezelon, pp. 127, 131. Volunteer with Brambley
Hedge Rabbit Rescue.

Valerie Fox, pp. 57, 68. Valerie shares her life with one
much-loved bun.

Stephen Guida, pp. 34, 83, 86, 141, 150. Volunteer with
Brambley Hedge Rabbit Rescue.

Timiae Harper, pp. 27, 31 (French Angora), 32. Crazzy
H Rabbitry. http://crazzyhrabbitry.homestead.com/

John Mead, p. 31 (English Spot). John shares his life with
his best friend/ wife, six cats, three rabbits, and one large
dog, all rescues.

Janelle Newbypp. 26 (Jersey Wooly, Lionheads), 71.
24carrotbunz, AR. Lionheads and Jersey Wooly. Although
Janelle primarily keeps her rabbits as pets, she occasionally
has young rabbits for sale. cte66762@centurytel.net

Velly Oliver, p. 13. Volunteer with Brambley Hedge Rabbit
Rescue.

Sunny Oaks Flemish Giants, pp. 35, 78, 165, 200.
http://sunnyoaksrabbits.tripod.com/

Everett White, pp. 49, 69, 125, 188. Everett and his wife,
Melissa, share their home with two house rabbits,
Peanutbutter and Flower.

bibliography

Anderson, C.O., V.H. Denenberg, and M.X. Zarrow. 1972. Effects of handling and social isolation upon the rabbit's behavior. *Behav.* 43: 165-175.

Anderson, Gail. 2000. Miniwheat: life with a senior rabbit. *The Bunny Thymes* 5(24): 11, 12.

Anonymous. 2003. Baby brown: a case history. *Rabbit Sanctuary Newsletter* Spring.

Atkins, Laura. 2000. A healthy house rabbit diet. *Rabbits* 5: 98-103.

Brown, Susan A. 1999. The importance of analgesia for pet rabbits. *Missouri House Rabbit Society Newsletter* 2(1).

BSAVA Manual of Rabbit Medicine and Surgery. 2000. Edited by Paul Flecknell. Gloucester: British Small Animal Veterinary Association.

BSAVA Manual of Small Animal Neurology. Second edition. 1995. Edited by Simon J. Wheeler. Cheltenham: British Small Animal Veterinary Association.

Carrow, Catherine. 2000. Safe and sound. *Rabbits* 5: 42-53.

Castanon, S., M.S. Marin, J.M. Martin-Alonso, J.M. Boga, R. Casais, J.M. Humara, R.J. Ordas, and F. Parra. 1999. Immunization with potato plants expressing VP90 Protein protects against rabbit hemorrhagic disease virus. *J.Virol.* 73(5): 4452-4455.

Coffin, J.M. and D.S. Woodruff-Pak. 1993. Delay classical conditioning in young and older rabbits: initial acquisition and retention at 12 and 18 months. *Behav. Neuro.* 107(1): 63-71.

Cotter, Mary E. 2003. Help! My bunny's sick. *Rabbits USA* 8: 39-48.

Cowan, David P. 1987. Aspects of the social organization of the European wild rabbit (*Oryctolagus cuniculus*). *Ethology* 75: 197-210.
Crook, Sandy. 1986. *Lops as Pets*. Neptune City: T.F.H. Publications, Inc.

Downes, Anne. 2000. Maintaining physical and psychological health in your rabbit. *The Bunny Thymes* 5(21):8.

Dubey, J.P. 1976. A review of *Sarcocystis* of domestic animals and of other coccidia of cats and dogs. *JAVMA* 169: 1061-1078.

DiGiacomo, R.F., L.E. Garlinghouse, G.L. Van Hoosier. 1983. Natural history of infection with *Pasteurella multocida* in rabbits. JAVMA 183 (11): 1172-1175.

The European Rabbit: The history and biology of a successful colonizer. 1994. Edited by Harry V. Thompson and Carolyn M. King. Oxford: Oxford U. Press.

Evans, George Ewart and David Thomson. 1972. *The Leaping Hare.* London: Faber and Faber Ltd.

Ezpeleta, Alicia. 1996. *Rabbits Everywhere.* New York: Harry N. Abhrams, Inc.

Feldman, K.A. 2003. Tularemia. *JAVMA* 222(6): 725-30.

Fiorello, C.V. and R.Z. German. 1997. Heterochrony within species: craniofacial growth in giant, standard, and dwarf rabbits. *Evolution* 51(1): 250-261.

Fox, R.R. and D.D. Crary. 1971. Mandibular prognathism in the rabbit: genetic studies. *J. Hered.* 62: 23-27.

Fritzche, Helga. 1977. *Rabbits*. New York: Barron's Educational Series, Inc.

Genetics and the Behavior of Domestic Animals. 1998. Edited by Temple Grandin. San Diego: Academic Press.

Gillett, N.A., D.L. Brooks, P.C. Tillman. 1983. Medical and surgical management of gastric obstruction from a hairball in the rabbit. *JAVMA* 183(11) 1176-1178.

Gonzalez-Mariscal, G., A.I. Melo, A. Zavala, and C. Beyer. 1992. Chin-marking behavior in male and female New Zealand rabbits: onset, development, and activation by steroids. *Physiology and Behavior* 52: 889-893.

Goodrich, B.S. and R. Mykytowycz. 1972. Individual and sex differences in the chemical composition of pheromone-like substances from the skin glands of the rabbit, *Oryctolagus cuniculus*. *J. Mammol.* 53: 540-548.

Graur, D., L. Duret, and M. Gouy. 1996. Phylogenetic position of the order Lagomorpha (rabbits, hares and allies). *Nature* 379(25): 333-335.

Guidry, Virginia Pack. 2000. What do you want in a rabbit? *Rabbits* 5: 64-73.

Harcourt-Brown, Frances. 2002. *Textbook of Rabbit Medicine.* Oxford: Butterworth-Heinemann.

Harkness, John E. and Joseph E. Wagner. Fourth edition. 1995. *The Biology and Medicine of Rabbits and Rodents.* London: Williams and Wilkins.

Harriman, Marinell. Third edition. 1995. *House Rabbit Handbook: How to Live with an Urban Rabbit.* Alameda: Drollery Press.

Hayes, R. A., B.J. Richardson, and S.G. Wylie. 2003. To fix or not to fix: the role of 2-phenoxyethanol in rabbit, *Oryctolagus cuniculus,* chin gland secretions. *J. Chem. Ecol.* 29(5): 1051-1064.

Hesterman, E.R., K. Malafant, and R. Mykytowycz. 1984. Misidentification by wild rabbits, *Oryctolagus cuniculus,* of group members carrying the odor of foreign inguinal gland secretion. *J. Chem. Ecol.* 10(3): 403-419.

Hyman's Comparative Vertebrate Anatomy. Third edition. 1992. Edited by Marvalee H. Wake. Chicago: University of Chicago Press.

Kazacos, K.R., W.M. Reed, E.A. Kazacos, and H.L. Thacker. 1983. Fatal cerebrospinal disease caused by *Baylisascaris procyonis* in domestic rabbits. *JAVMA* 183(9): 967-971.

Kennedy, G.A., R. Hudson, and S.M. Armstrong. 1994. Circadian wheel running activity rhythms in two strains of domestic rabbit. *Phys. and Behav.* 55(2): 385-389.

King, James. 1986. *William Cowper: A Biography.* Durham: Duke U. Press.

Kolb, H.H. 1992. The effect of moonlight on activity in the wild rabbit (*Oryctolagus cuniculus*). *J. Zool.* 228: 661-665.

Laska, Matthias. 2002. Gustatory responsiveness to food-associated saccharides in European rabbits, *Oryctolagus cuniculus. Phys. and Behav.* 76: 335-341.

Leverett, Brian. 1987. *Keeping Rabbits: a complete manual.* London: Blandford Press.

Lockley, R.M. 1961. Social structure and stress in the rabbit warren. *J. Anim.* Eco. 30(2): 385-423.

McBride, Anne. 1998. *Why does my rabbit . . . ?* London: Souvenir Press.

McLaughlin, Marie L. 1916. *Myths and Legends of the Sioux.* Reprint, Lincoln: University of Nebraska Press, 1990.

The Merck Veterinary Manual. Eighth edition. 1998. Edited by Susan E. Aiello. Whitehouse Station: Merck and Co., Inc.

Miller, C. D. 1998. Happily ever after. *Cats* 54(4): 38-42.

Millichamp, N.J. and B.R. Collins. 1986. Blepharoconjunctivitis associated with *Staphylococcus aureus* in a rabbit. *JAVMA* 189(9):1153-1154.

Moustaki, Nikki. 2003. Nibble this. *Rabbits* USA 8: 12-19.

Murray, Jill. 2000. Beyond disability there is life. *The Bunny Thymes* 5(24): 6-9.

Mykytowycz, R. 1968. Territorial marking by rabbits. *Sci. Amer.* 218(5): 116-126.

Ordinola, P., M. Martinez–Gomez, J. Manzo, and R. Hudson. 1997. Response of male domestic rabbits (*Oryctolagus cuniculus*) to inguinal gland secretion from intact and ovariectomized females. *J. Chem. Ecol.* 23(9): 2079-2091.

Pavia, Audrey. 2000. Actions speak louder than words. *Rabbits* 5: 98-103.

Rahman, Ifsha. 2001. Animal encounters of the safe kind. *Rabbits* 6:36-43.

Robinson, D. 1979. *The Encyclopedia of Pet Rabbits*. Hong Kong: T.F.H. Publications, Inc.

Rohrbach, B.W. 1988. Tularemia. *JAVMA* 193(4): 428-432.

Shell, L.G. and G. Saounders. 1989. Arteriosclerosis in a rabbit. *JAVMA* 194(5):679-680.

Shuffstall, Sandy Koi. 2000. Elderbuns. *The Bunny Thymes.* 5(22):1-7.

Smith, Kathy. 2001. *Rabbit Health in the 21st Century: A Guide for Bunny Parents*. Kansas City: Kathy Smith.

Smith, Susan. 2000. Caring for the invalid rabbit. *The Bunny Thymes* 5(24): 6-9.

Swartout, M.S. and D.F. Gerken. 1987. Lead-induced toxicosis in two domestic rabbits. *JAVMA* 191 (6): 717-719.

Taylor, Judy. 1996. *Beatrix Potter: Artist, Storyteller, and Countrywoman*. Second edition. London: Frederick Warne.

Thilsted, J.P., W.M. Newton, R.A. Crandell, and R.F. Bevill. 1981. Fatal diarrhea in rabbits resulting from the feeding of antibiotic-contaminated feed. *JAVMA* 179: 360, 361.

Tyrell, Kerin L., Diane M. Citron, Jeffrey R. Jenkins, Ellie J.C. Goldstein, and Veterinary Study Group. 2002. Periodontal bacteria in rabbit mandibular and maxillary abscesses. *J. Clin. Micro.* 40(3): 1044-1047.

Vriends-Parent, Lucia. 1989. *The New Rabbit Handbook*. Huappage: Barron's Educational Series.

Wegler, Monika. 1985. *Dwarf Rabbits*. Huappage: Barron's Educational Series.

Wheat, C.K. 2001. Abscesses in rabbits. *Rabbit Sanctuary Newsletter* Spring.

Wheat, C. K. 2001. Dental problems in rabbits. *Rabbit Sanctuary Newsletter* Summer.

Wissman, Margaret A. 2000. Rabbit medicine. *Rabbits* 5: 18-29.

Yu, B. and H.Y. Tsen. 1993. Lactobacillus cells in the rabbit digestive tract and the factors affecting their distribution. *J. App. Bact.* 75:269-275.

Zeuner, Frederick E. 1963. *A History of Domesticated Animals*. London: Hutchison and Co. Ltd.

index

Books Available from Santa Monica Press

American Hydrant
by Sean Crane
176 pages $24.95

The Book of Good Habits
*Simple and Creative Ways to
Enrich Your Life*
by Dirk Mathison
224 pages $9.95

The Butt Hello
*and other ways my cats
drive me crazy*
by Ted Meyer
96 pages $9.95

Childish Things
by Davis & Davis
96 pages $19.95

**Discovering the History of
Your House**
and Your Neighborhood
by Betsy J. Green
288 pages $14.95

The Dog Ate My Resumé
by Zack Arnstein and Larry
Arnstein
192 pages $11.95

Dogme Uncut
*Lars von Trier, Thomas Vinterberg
and the Gang That Took on
Hollywood*
by Jack Stevenson
312 pages $16.95

**Exotic Travel Destinations
for Families**
by Jennifer M. Nichols
and Bill Nichols
360 pages $16.95

Footsteps in the Fog
Alfred Hitchcock's San Francisco
by Jeff Kraft and
Aaron Leventhal
240 pages $24.95

**Free Stuff & Good Deals
for Folks over 50, 2nd Ed.**
by Linda Bowman
240 pages $12.95

A House Rabbit Primer
by Lucile C. Moore
264 pages $14.95

**How to Find Your Family
Roots and Write Your
Family History**
by William Latham and
Cindy Higgins
288 pages $14.95

How to Speak Shakespeare
by Cal Pritner and
Louis Colaianni
144 pages $16.95

**How to Win Lotteries,
Sweepstakes, and Contests in
the 21st Century, 2nd Edition**
by Steve "America's
Sweepstakes King" Ledoux
224 pages $14.95

**Jackson Pollock:
Memories Arrested in Space**
by Martin Gray
216 pages $14.95

James Dean Died Here
*The Locations of America's Pop
Culture Landmarks*
by Chris Epting
312 pages $16.95

The Keystone Kid
Tales of Early Hollywood
by Coy Watson, Jr.
312 pages $24.95

**The Largest U.S. Cities
Named after a Food**
by Brandt Maxwell
360 pages $16.95

Letter Writing Made Easy!
*Featuring Sample Letters for
Hundreds of Common Occasions*
by Margaret McCarthy
224 pages $12.95

**Letter Writing Made Easy!
Volume 2**
*Featuring More Sample Letters for
Hundreds of Common Occasions*
by Margaret McCarthy
224 pages $12.95

Life is Short. Eat Biscuits!
by Amy Jordan Smith
96 pages $9.95

Loving Through Bars
Children with Parents in Prison
by Cynthia Martone
208 pages $21.95

Marilyn Monroe Dyed Here
*More Locations of America's
Pop Culture Landmarks*
by Chris Epting
312 pages $16.95

Movie Star Homes
by Judy Artunian and
Mike Oldham
312 pages $16.95

Offbeat Museums
*The Collections and Curators of
America's Most Unusual Museums*
by Saul Rubin
240 pages $19.95

A Prayer for Burma
by Kenneth Wong
216 pages $14.95

Quack!
*Tales of Medical Fraud from
the Museum of Questionable
Medical Devices*
by Bob McCoy
240 pages $19.95

Redneck Haiku
by Mary K. Witte
112 pages $9.95

**School Sense: How to Help
Your Child Succeed in
Elementary School**
by Tiffani Chin, Ph.D.
408 pages $16.95

Silent Echoes
*Discovering Early Hollywood
Through the Films of
Buster Keaton*
by John Bengtson
240 pages $24.95

Tiki Road Trip
*A Guide to Tiki Culture
in North America*
by James Teitelbaum
288 pages $16.95